# All-in-One Bible Fun

## Heroes of the Bible

*Elementary*

# Also available from Abingdon Press

## All-in-One Bible Fun

### Fruit of the Spirit
*Preschool*

### Fruit of the Spirit
*Elementary*

### Stories of Jesus
*Preschool*

### Stories of Jesus
*Elementary*

### Favorite Bible Stories
*Preschool*

### Favorite Bible Stories
*Elementary*

### Heroes of the Bible
*Preschool*

Writers/Editors: LeeDell Stickler, Daphna Flegal
Production Editors: Anna Raitt, Billie Brownell
Production and Design Manager: Marcia C'deBaca
Illustrator: Megan Jeffery
Cover photo: jupiterimages

# All-in-One

# BIBLE

# FUN

## Heroes of the Bible
### Elementary

ABINGDON PRESS
Nashville

All-in-One Bible Fun
Heroes of the Bible
Elementary

ISBN 9781426707810

10 11 12 13 14 15 16 17 18 19 - 10 9 8 7 6 5 4 3 2 1

MANUFACTURED IN THE UNITED STATES OF AMERICA

# All-in-One BIBLE FUN Table of Contents

# Bible Units in *Heroes of the Bible*

*Use these suggestions if you choose to organize the lessons in short-term units.*

## Old Testament Heroes

| Bible Story | Bible Verse |
|---|---|
| Daniel | The name of the LORD is to be praised. Psalm 113:3 |
| Jonah | Whoever loves God must love others also. 1 John 4:21, GNT |
| Joshua | For God all things are possible. Matthew 19:26 |
| Noah | I have set my bow in the clouds, and it shall be a sign of the covenant between me and the earth. Genesis 9:13 |
| David | If God is for us, who is against us? Romans 8:31 |
| Miriam and Moses | Love one another as I have loved you. John 15:12 |
| Esther | Be strong, and let your heart take courage. Psalm 27:14 |

## New Testament Heroes

| Bible Story | Bible Verse |
|---|---|
| Jesus and the Children | Let the little children come to me; do not stop them; for it is to such as these that the kingdom of God belongs. Mark 10:14 |
| A Boy and His Lunch | Do not neglect to do good and to share what you have, for such sacrifices are pleasing to God. Hebrews 13:16 |
| Peter and John | Just as you did it to one of the least of these who are members of my family, you did it to me. Matthew 25:40 |
| Dorcas | Trust in the LORD and do good. Psalm 37:3 |
| Paul | Do not be afraid . . . for I am with you. Acts 18:9-10 |
| Lydia | We are ambassadors for Christ. 2 Corinthians 5:20 |

# Supplies

(This is a comprehensive list of all the supplies needed if you choose to do all the activities. It is your choice whether your group will do all the activities.)

- Bibles
- crayons, glitter crayons
- colored pencils
- pencils
- ruler
- cotton balls or bathroom issue
- shower rings or large metal washers
- paper clips
- plastic toy
- basket
- watercolor and permanent felt-tip markers
- construction paper
- posterboard
- scissors, safety scissors
- masking tape and clear tape
- water color paints, paint brushes
- cups of water
- smocks
- table covering
- newspaper
- cloth, purple cloth
- wooden craft sticks
- rubber bands
- stapler, staples
- yarn
- crepe paper
- white glue
- plastic tub
- trash can
- drawing paper
- water color paper

- scarfs/blindfolds/bandannas
- large paper grocery bags
- large-size paper
- balls, foam balls
- beach ball or balloon
- towel
- box
- sheets or fabric
- Bible-times costumes
- bag of clothing
- dominoes
- clean-up supplies: spray cleaner, sponges, paper towels
- book
- magnet
- chair
- rocks
- paper punch
- dress-up/decorative accessories
- beanbag

# Welcome to All-in-One Bible Fun

Have fun learning about heroes of the Bible. Each lesson in this teacher guide is filled with games and activities that will make learning fun for you and your children. With just a few added supplies, everything you need to teach is included in Abingdon's *All-in-One Bible Fun*. Each lesson has a box with a picture of a cookie,

> # We can tell others about Jesus.

that is repeated over and over again throughout the lesson. The cookie box states the Bible message in words your children will understand.

## Use the following tips to help make *All-in-One Bible Fun* a success!

- Read through each lesson. Read the Bible passages.
- Memorize the Bible verse and the cookie box statement.
- Choose activities that fit your unique group of children and your time limitations. If time is limited, we recommend those activities noted in **boldface** on the chart page and by a *balloon* beside each activity.

*balloon symbol*

- Practice telling the Bible story.
- Gather supplies you will use for the lesson.
- Learn the music included in each lesson. All the songs are written to familiar tunes.
- Arrange your room space to fit the lesson. Move tables and chairs so there is plenty of room for the children to move and to sit on the floor.
- Copy the Reproducible pages for the lesson.

# Elementary

Each child in your class is a one-of-a-kind child of God. Each child has his or her own name, background, family situation, and set of experiences. It is important to remember and celebrate the uniqueness of each child. Yet these one-of-a-kind children of God have some common needs.

- All children need love.
- All children need a sense of self-worth.
- All children need to feel a sense of accomplishment.
- All children need to have a safe place to be and express their feelings.
- All children need to be surrounded by adults who love them.
- All children need to experience the love of God.

**Younger elementary children (ages 6-10 years old) also have some common characteristics.**

## Their Bodies

- They are growing at different rates.
- They are energetic, restless, and have difficulty sitting still.
- They are developing fine motor skills.
- They want to participate rather than watch or listen.

## Their Minds

- They are developing basic academic skills.
- They are eager to learn new things.
- They learn best by working imaginatively and creatively.
- They have little sense of time.
- They are concrete thinkers and cannot interpret symbols.
- They are developing an ability to reason and discuss.
- They like to have a part in planning their own activities.

## Their Relationships

- They want to play with other children.
- They are sensitive to the feelings of others.
- They are shifting dependence from parents to teachers.
- They enjoy team activities but often dispute the rules.
- They imitate adults in attitudes and actions.

## Their Hearts

- They are open to learning about God.
- They need caring adults who model Christian behaviors.
- They need to sing, move to, and say Bible verses.
- They need to hear simple Bible stories.
- They can talk with God easily if encouraged.
- They are asking questions about God.
- They can share food and money and make things for others.

# Daniel

## Bible Verse

The name of the LORD is to be praised.

Psalm 113:3

## Bible Story

Daniel 6:1-28

Daniel was a Hebrew man who as a boy was taken into exile by the Babylonians. As a security measure, the Babylonian army carried away from their homeland those men, women, and children whom they had conquered, transplanting them far away. This lessened the likelihood that those who were left would rise up against their conquerors.

In today's Bible story, Daniel is trying to remain faithful to God while living in a land far from the Temple of Jerusalem. Daniel, obviously a man of great talent and integrity, caught the eye of King Darius. The king put Daniel in a high position within the Babylonian government. Being in a high profile position was often dangerous, especially for a foreigner such as Daniel. Other people who were at the same position level as Daniel resented him. Consequently, they began to plot against Daniel. They knew of Daniel's great faithfulness to his religion and tried to use it as a way to get rid of him. Daniel discovered that it isn't easy to be faithful to God.

Once it could have been said that standing up for one's beliefs in today's world would have rarely resulted in physical injury. But if we look at the world in which many of our children live, we see that this is no longer the case. Consider the number of handguns and other weapons that make their way into the public schools in the course of a year— even the elementary schools.

We call our children to be faithful to God. This sounds so simple, yet it is not. Once, attending church on Sunday was the rule, now it is the exception. Children's sporting events are regularly scheduled on Sundays during church hours.

How do we, as adults, help our children deal with the choices that they now face? Without adult guidance, many of our children will crumble under peer pressure. Support the children who attend your class. Give them the tools to make appropriate choices.

# It isn't always easy to be faithful to God.

If time is limited, we recommend those activities that are noted in **boldface**. Depending on your time and the number of children, you may be able to include more activities.

| ACTIVITY | TIME | SUPPLIES | |
|---|---|---|---|
| **Make Lion Puppets** | **10 minutes** | **Reproducible 1A, safety scissors, glue or tape, drawing paper, cardboard for backing** | JOIN THE FUN |
| Work Together | 10 minutes | masking tape; several items from your classroom such as a box of crayons, a toy, a book, glue, and markers | |
| Think Difficult | 5 minutes | None | BIBLE STORY FUN |
| Being Faithful | 5 minutes | large pieces of paper, felt-tip markers | |
| **Bible Story: Faithful Daniel** | **10 minutes** | **lion puppets (Reproducible 1A)** | |
| Do the Daniel Hop | 10 minutes | optional: lion puppets (Reproducible 1A) | |
| Let's Be Faithful | 10 minutes | Reproducible 1B, scissors | LIVE THE FUN |
| **Body Prayers** | **5 minutes** | **Bible** | |

# JOIN THE FUN

# Make Lion Puppets

Greet the children warmly as they come into the room. Photocopy one lion puppet (**Reproducible 1A**) for each child.

Let each child color, cut out, and assemble the lion puppet (**Reproducible 1A**) according to the directions. Let the children add small bits of cardboard to the back of each piece before gluing it to the base. This makes the puppet three dimensional. Fold a piece of drawing paper over and over. Use this as the base for the puppet. Let the children put their names on the completed puppets and put them in the storytelling area.

# Work Together

Use the masking tape to make a circle or square on the floor. Then make a circle or square of similar size about ten feet away. Place several items from your classroom (a box of crayons, a toy, a book, glue, markers) in one of the areas. Have the children stand in a line.

Say: **The object of this game is to move each item from one area to the other area—one item at a time. Each person has one minute. When the minute is over, I will shout, "Next!" and the next person takes over.**

Designate one child as the beginning player. Then as if you just happened to remember,

Say: **Get ready, get set, oh, wait a minute. I forgot to tell you. There's a catch. You can't use your hands. Now go!**

Allow each child 30 to 60 seconds; then shout, "Next!" Then the next child gets to try. Play until each child has had an opportunity to try to move the items. Have the children sit down in a circle.

Ask: **At first, did this game seem to be easy? What made it hard? How did you feel when you couldn't use your hands?**

Say: **In today's Bible story, we have a man who is faced with doing something very difficult. He is called upon to be faithful, but he's having a hard time.**

**It isn't always easy to be faithful to God.**

# Think Difficult

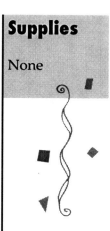

Ask: **What is the most difficult thing you can think of to do?**

Have the children take turns and act it out. Let the other class members try to guess. Give the children a minute or two to come up with something such as climbing a mountain, driving a car, doing math problems, cleaning windows, or practicing the piano.

Say: **In today's Bible story a man named Daniel has to do something very, very hard. He has to choose whether or not to be faithful to God. That doesn't seem very difficult, but it is.**

> **It isn't always easy to be faithful to God.**

# Being Faithful

Ask: **What does the word *faithful* mean?** *(loyal)* **If we are faithful to God, what does that mean?** *(being loyal to God)* **What kinds of things would we do to show that we are loyal/faithful to God?**

Say: **Let's make a list.**

Write the children's suggestions on the paper. You may want to give some initial suggestions such as pray, read the Bible, go to Sunday school and church, be kind to others, tell others about Jesus, give an offering to church, or follow the Ten Commandments.

Ask: **Do you think being faithful would be difficult or easy? What would happen if someone passed a law that said you couldn't do any of those things? What would happen if I ordered you to get up from the floor, but that it was against the law to use your hands?**

Have the children cross their arms across their chest and try to stand up.

Ask: **Is that easy or hard? Is that a silly rule? What if I said that in order to be faithful to God you had to eat liver every morning for breakfast? Would that be difficult to do?**

Say: **In today's Bible story, some jealous government officials convince the king to make a law that was just as silly.**

**13**

# Faithful Daniel

by LeeDell Stickler

> Have the children use their lion puppets from the "Make Lion Puppets" activity (**Reproducible 1A**) as you tell the story.
>
> **Say: I am going to tell the story, but I need your help. Every time you hear the word** *faithful*, **I want to hear the lions roar. Let me hear you roar.** *(Let the children roar.)* **You don't sound hungry enough. Let me hear you roar again.**

Once, a long, long time ago, in a land very far away, there was a king named Darius [duh RI uhs] This king had many court officials who helped him to run the country. One of these court officials was a man named Daniel. Unlike the other court officials, Daniel was a foreigner. But he was honest and a hard worker. He was also **faithful** to the one true God.

Because Daniel was such a hard worker, the king made Daniel head of all the other court officials. This did not make these officials very happy. In fact, they were very jealous. They began to look for a way to make Daniel look bad in the eyes of the king. But as hard as they tried, they could find nothing wrong with Daniel. Daniel was kind and good and honest. Daniel was **faithful** to his God.

Then, one day, one of the court officials had an idea. "If we are going to get Daniel in trouble, we'll have to somehow use his religion. I have seen him go up to his room three times a day to pray to God. Suppose we have the king make a law that says it is illegal to pray to anyone but the king. Daniel will never follow such a law. He is very **faithful** to his God."

The court officials went to the king. "O King Darius, may you live forever. We have decided that you should make a special law. No one is to pray to anyone except the king for the next thirty days. Anyone who breaks the law will be thrown into a den of hungry lions. And this law will be one that even the king cannot break."

ALL-IN-ONE BIBLE FUN

"Done!" said the king, as he signed the law into being. The court officials smiled little secret smiles. Now they wondered just what **faithful** Daniel would do.

Daniel knew about the new law. But Daniel was **faithful** to God. And God's law said that Daniel was to pray to God three times a day and not to pray to anyone else. Daniel certainly didn't want to disobey the king's law, but he also didn't want to disobey God's law, either. So, just as he had always done, three times a day, **faithful** Daniel went to his room to pray.

This pleased the court officials. Now they could get Daniel into trouble. When the officials told the king what Daniel was doing, the king was sad. He truly liked Daniel. He didn't want to throw Daniel into a den of hungry lions. But the law was the law, and even the king could not change it.

So, **faithful** Daniel was thrown into the den of hungry lions. "May your God protect you," said the king, as men rolled the stone across the mouth of the den. And King Darius went back to his palace.

But there was no sleep for King Darius that night. He tossed and turned. He turned and tossed. All he could think about was his friend Daniel and those hungry lions.

When morning came, the king rushed to where they had left Daniel. "Daniel?" he called out. "Can you hear me?"

Then Daniel called out to the king, "I am here, O King. God sent an angel to shut the lions' mouths so that they would not hurt me. I am safe because I have done no wrong."

Then King Darius wrote to all the peoples who lived within his kingdom, "The God to whom Daniel is **faithful** is the one and true God. And God's kingdom shall have no end."

## Supplies

optional: lion puppets (Reproducible 1A)

# Do the Daniel Hop

**Say:** In today's Bible story, Daniel decides to be faithful to God, even though it means going against the king's law.

> ## It isn't always easy to be faithful to God.

Have the children stand in a line, one behind the other. Ask them to hold both hands up like a lion's paws. (Option: Use the lion puppets instead.)

Use these motions with the chant: hop up and extend right foot out. Hop up and return right foot to original position. Repeat. Use the same actions for the left foot. Hop forward. Hop backward. Hop forward three hops (at the words "roar, roar, roar"). Repeat for each verse of the poem.

The teacher should say the first three lines, the children will repeat the fourth line as they hop forward.

> In a land so far away,
> There lived a man who liked to pray,
> Prayed to God three times a day.
> Roar, roar, roar.
>
> Some jealous men dreamed up a plan,
> And sent a law throughout the land,
> Decreeing prayers to God were banned.
> Roar, roar, roar.
>
> But Daniel chose to do what's right
> And in his room within plain sight,
> He prayed to God both day and night.
> Roar, roar, roar.
>
> Daniel was the king's good friend,
> But still was put into the den,
> Because of other jealous men.
> Roar, roar, roar.
>
> With lions Daniel spent the night.
> The king rushed down at morning's light,
> To find that Daniel was all right!
> Roar, roar, roar.

# Let's Be Faithful

Photocopy and cut apart the action cards **(Reproducible 1B)**. Place the cards face down on the table or in a basket or box.

Let each child choose an action card. One at a time let the children read the action on the card. Then have the class decide whether the action is one where a child has been faithful to God or not. If the action is faithful, have the children stand up and cheer. If the action is not faithful, have the children cover their faces and groan, "Oh, no."

**Ask: Can you think of a time when you had to make a choice between obeying God's laws and doing what other people want you to do? When no one sees you do something wrong, does it make it all right? Besides you, who will know when you do something wrong?** (God)

**Say: Chances are, if we are not faithful to God, today we will NOT be thrown into a den of lions. You might think it would be easier to be faithful to God today, but sometimes it is really harder. We come to church to learn what it means to be faithful to God.**

# Body Prayers

**Say: One way Daniel was faithful to God was that he prayed to God three times a day—in the morning, at noon, and at night.**

**Ask: What do you think he said to God? What do you say to God? Do you say thank you for food and friends? Do you say thank you for family and fun?**

Have a child find and read the Bible verse, "The name of the LORD is to be praised" (Psalm 113:3), from the Bible.

**Say: Today we are going to close with a body prayer. Praising God through prayer is one way to be faithful. As we say the words, we will use certain motions.**

**We praise you, God,**—hands come to the center to form praying hands and move up and out, extending over head.
**In the morning**—put both hands beside face, fingers outstretched making a smiling morning face.
**We praise you, God,**—repeat first action.
**In the evening**—place hands together, under side of face and pretend to sleep.
**We praise you, God,**—repeat first action.
**All the time**—hands outstretched, turn all the way around.
**Amen.**—fold hands in prayer.

**17**

### REPRODUCIBLE 1A

ALL-IN-ONE BIBLE FUN

| | |
|---|---|
| tell a lie | sing in the choir |
| say your prayers | use God's name in a bad way |
| read the Bible | be kind to others |
| share with a friend | steal from someone |
| obey your parents | give an offering to the poor |
| go to church | hit a classmate at school |
| cheat on a test | make a card for a sick friend |
| donate food to a food pantry | be in a walk for the homeless |

All-in-One
**BIBLE** ELEMENTARY
**FUN**

# Jonah

## Bible Verse

Whoever loves God must love others also.

1 John 4:21, GNT

## Bible Story

Jonah 1–2

Nineveh was the capital of the Assyrian empire. The Assyrians were longtime enemies of the people of Judah. Why would Jonah, a devout Jew, want to preach God's forgiveness to a nation that had so oppressed his country? Nothing could have been more distasteful! But this was exactly what God told Jonah to do. Jonah, on the other hand, had other ideas. However, God's will prevailed.

The Book of Jonah comes from the period of Jewish history known as post-Exilic. Around the fifth century B.C., the Jewish people had begun to return to their homeland after being exiled in Babylonia. Among the political leaders there was a sense of nationalism and racial exclusivity. They wanted to recreate an exclusive Jewish community, free of outside influence. The Book of Jonah, however, preached the responsibility of God's chosen people to bear witness to God, whose love and forgiveness was to all people. A man named

Jesus, who appeared many years later, confirmed this message.

Children are naturally very loving and accepting. When encouraged, they are willing to include everyone in their activities. Most of their prejudices and exclusive behaviors are those that they have learned from an older peer group or from adults. Set an example of acceptance in your classroom. Discourage children from forming cliques that leave other children out. Plan games that encourage participation from all the children, games that foster cooperation and not competition.

The church welcomes all people, just as Jesus welcomed all people. Welcoming others does not mean that we teach our children to be reckless when coming into contact with people they do not know. But wholesale rejection on the basis of religion, skin color, gender, or any other qualification is not acceptable.

# God's love is for everyone.

If time is limited, we recommend those activities that are noted in **boldface**. Depending on your time and the number of children, you may be able to include more activities.

| ACTIVITY | TIME | SUPPLIES | |
|---|---|---|---|
| **Go Fishing** | **10 minutes** | **Reproducible 2A, cotton balls or facial tissue, stapler, staples, scissors, crayons or felt-tip markers, paper clips, yarn, crepe paper, tape, paper punch** | JOIN THE FUN |
| Keep Out! | 10 minutes | ball | BIBLE STORY FUN |
| Set the Stage | 5 minutes | None | |
| **Bible Story: Jonah and the Fish** | **10 minutes** | **None** | |
| Who Swallowed Jonah? | 10 minutes | Reproducible 2B, stapler, staples, safety scissors, masking tape, crayons or felt-tip markers, rubber bands (about three to four inches long) | |
| Bible Verse Bounce | 10 minutes | ball, towel | |
| Fish for Partners | 5 minutes | fish (Reproducible 2A), cardboard box, yarn, magnet | LIVE THE FUN |
| **Friendship Prayers** | **5 minutes** | **None** | |

# JOIN THE FUN

## Supplies

Reproducible 2A, cotton balls or facial tissue, stapler, staples, safety scissors, crayons or felt-tip markers, paper clips yarn, crepe paper, tape, paper punch

# Go Fishing

Before the children arrive, cut crepe paper into streamers and tape them to the doorway. Let the streamers hang down and blow about like a waterfall.

Then cut additional streamers from yarn about six to eight feet long. Attach partially opened paper clips to the yarn, forming a hook. Tape the yarn to the ceiling. When the children finish their name fish **(Reproducible 2A)**, let them hang the fish from the ceiling in the storytelling area.

Photocopy two fish **(Reproducible 2A)** for each child.

Greet the children warmly as they arrive. Let them share any events that have happened since the last time you saw them. If you have new students, let them make nametags.

**Ask: Do you notice anything special about our room today? What do the streamers remind you of?** *(water, ocean, waves)* **What do you think today's Bible story is going to be about? Can you think of any Bible stories that have to do with the ocean?**

Give each child two fish **(Reproducible 2A)**. Have each child write her or his name somewhere on each fish. Let the children decorate their fish with crayons or markers.

Then have the child cut out both fish and stack the them together with the decorated sides facing out. Help the children staple the fish together around the edges, leaving the top open.

Encourage each child to stuff the fish with cotton balls or facial tissue and then staple the open edge together. Punch a hole in the top fin.

Show the child how to attach a paper clip to the top fin. Hang the fish from one of the hooks from the ceiling.

**Say: In today's Bible story we meet a man named Jonah. He learns a very important message.**

> ## God's love is for everyone.

# Keep Out!

Bring the children together in an open space for a game. Move all the furniture to the side. Select several children to be in the center of the group. The rest should form a circle around them.

The object of the game is for the players in the outer circle to pass the ball back and forth so that the players (or player) in the inner circle cannot get the ball. If a player in the inner circle catches the ball, he or she trades places with the person who passed it. When the game is over, have the children sit down right where they are.

**Ask: How did it feel to have the ball? How did it feel not to have the ball? How did it feel to know that people were trying to keep you from getting the ball?**

**Say: In today's Bible story we meet a man named Jonah. He learns a very important lesson. He learns that God's love doesn't leave anyone out; God's love is for everyone.**

# Set the Stage

**Say: Did you know that long ago in Bible times, some people felt that God belonged only to them? They didn't want God to love anyone who wasn't one of them. They didn't want God to forgive anyone who wasn't one of them. They wanted to keep God all to themselves. Do you think God belongs to only certain people? No! God's love is for everyone!**

Have the children repeat the following phrase after you: "God's love is for everyone." Begin by saying the phrase in a whisper, gradually getting louder and louder.

**Say: Today's story is about a man who thought of himself as a good man. He lived the way he felt God wanted him to live. But he learned a very important lesson.**

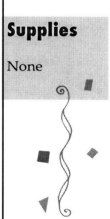

## Supplies

ball

## Supplies

None

 God's love is for everyone.

# Jonah and the Fish

by LeeDell Stickler

Tell the story dramatically. Do the suggested movements and encourage the children to do the movements with you.

A long time ago, there lived a man named Jonah. *(Hands on your hips.)* Jonah was a good man.

And Jonah said: *(Pause.)*
I always want to do what's right
I want to be faithful and true.
I try to live as God would like
And do what God wants me to.

One day God spoke to Jonah. *(Shake finger at the children as if you are instructing them.)* "Jonah, I want you to go to the city of Nineveh. Tell the people there how wicked they are. I want them to change their wicked ways. If they don't, they will be very sorry." *(Shake head sadly.)*

And Jonah said: *(Pause dramatically.)*
I always want to do what's right
I want to be faithful and true.
I try to live as God would like
But this I will not do. *(Shake head.)*

Jonah did not like the people of Nineveh. *(Hold both arms out in front as if pushing someone away.)* They were his enemies. So, instead of going to Nineveh, Jonah boarded a ship that was going in the opposite direction.

And Jonah said: *(Pause dramatically.)*
I always want to do what's right.
I want to be faithful and true.
But now I'm going to run away,
That's just what I will do.

So, Jonah got onto the ship. *(Walk as if going up a gangplank.)* Jonah went below and promptly fell asleep. *(Put head on hands as if asleep. Make snoring sounds.)* While Jonah was sound asleep, the boat set sail. *(Wave goodbye.)* As it sailed, a great storm came up. *(Have the children rock back and forth as though they are the boat.)* The wind blew. The lightning flashed. The waves crashed against the ship. Everyone feared the boat would sink. *(Everyone pretends to hold onto the sides of the boat and rock back and forth.)*

ALL-IN-ONE BIBLE FUN

The captain woke Jonah up. "How can you sleep in such a storm? Pray to your God that we might not all be killed."

And Jonah said: *(Pause dramatically.)*
I always want to do what's right.
I want to be faithful and true.
But when I ran away from God,
I brought this trouble for you.

So, Jonah told the sailors, "Throw me into the sea and the storm will come to an end." *(Encourage the children to pretend to row a boat. Say: Faster, faster! We're sinking!)* The sailors did not want Jonah to drown. So, instead, they rowed with all their might. But the storm just got worse and worse.

And Jonah said: *(Pause dramatically.)*
I always want to do what's right.
I want to be faithful and true.
Throw me into the deep, dark sea
That's just what you must do.

Finally, the sailors picked Jonah up and threw him over the side. As soon as Jonah hit the water, the storm stopped. *(Pause.)* And up from the deep, dark depths of the ocean came a big fish. The fish opened its mouth and swallowed Jonah whole. *(Hold arms apart as though a big mouth and then snap shut.)*

And Jonah said: *(Pause dramatically.)*
I always want to do what's right.
I want to be faithful and true.
Now here I am in the belly of a fish,
Feeling sad and blue.

For three days Jonah sat there in the belly of that fish. *(Drum fingers on the leg as if in boredom.)* For three days Jonah prayed to God. *(Fold hands in prayer.)*

And Jonah said: *(Pause dramatically.)*
I always want to do what's right.
I want to be faithful and true.
Whatever job you have for me,
Then that is what I'll do.

The fish came to the surface of the water and spit Jonah onto the dry land. And do you know what Jonah did next? He went to Ninevah. And do you know what the people of Nineveh did? They changed their ways. *(Applaud.)*

When God calls us to do special things, what should we say?

We always want do what's right.
We want to be faithful and true.
Whatever God should ask of us,
Then that is what we'll do.

## Supplies

Reproducible 2B, stapler, staples, safety scissors, masking tape, crayons or felt-tip markers, rubber bands (about three to four inches long)

# Who Swallowed Jonah?

Photocopy the Jonah figure and fish **(Reproducible 2B)** for each child.

Give each child the figures. Let the children color the fish and Jonah. Then have the children cut out the figures.

Show the children how to fold both Jonah and the fish figures on the dotted lines.

Help each child tape and/or staple one end of a rubber band inside Jonah. The remainder of the rubber band will hang out the foot end about two inches. Staple around the three open sides of the figure, and where the rubber band is taped.

Help each child place Jonah inside the folded fish so that only the tip of the head is showing through the fish's mouth.

Have each child open his or her fish. Help the child extend the rubber band without stretching and tape and/or staple the end down. Staple around the open edges of the fish. Staple through all thicknesses, catching the taped rubber band.

Show the children how to hold the fish so that your fingers are also on the taped end of the rubber band. Gently pull Jonah from the mouth of the fish. Then let go. Jonah will pop back in.

**Ask: When you pull Jonah out of the fish, what is he holding?** *(a heart)* **What does the heart say?** *(God's love is for everyone.)*

## Supplies

ball, towel

# Bible Verse Bounce

**Say: Let's play the "Keep Out" activity with the ball again. This time let's find a way to include all of us at the same time.**

Let each child gather around the towel, holding a part of the edge. Place the ball in the center of the towel. Let the children work together to bounce the ball up and down.

**Say: Let's say the Bible verse as we bounce the ball around. "Whoever loves God must love others also" (1 John 4:21, GNT).**

**Say: God didn't say love only people who have blond hair. God didn't say love only people who can play basketball. God didn't say love only people who smell good. God didn't say love only people who live on your street. God said love one another, and that means everyone!**

26

# Fish for Partners

**Supplies**

fish (Reproducible 2A), cardboard box, yarn, magnet

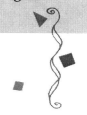

Attach a magnet to a three-foot length of yarn. Have the children get the fish they made in the "Go Fishing" activity. Put them in the box.

Say: One of the ways we show love to one another is to pray for one another. We're going to choose a prayer partner for the next week. But we are going to choose it in a special way.

Let each child "fish" for a prayer partner *(dropping the magnet on a fishing line to attract a "fish.")*. If a child catches his or her own name, have the child throw the fish back in the box and try again.

Say: Look at the name on the fish you caught. Remember to pray for this person during this next week.

# Friendship Prayers

**Supplies**

None

Ask: Have you ever known a person whom you really didn't like? Is there a person at school or in your neighborhood who, when you see him or her coming, you want to run away? Without saying his or her name aloud, think about that person now.

Say: We all have someone whom we don't like—someone who annoys us, someone who makes us feel uncomfortable. But the Bible says: "Whoever loves God must love others also" (1 John 4:21, GNT). Let's say that together.

*(Repeat the Bible verse.)* Let's say it again a little louder. *(Repeat the Bible verse a little louder.)*

Should we only love persons who live in our country?
Should we only love persons who go to our church?
Should we only love persons who have brown eyes?
Should we only love persons who wear *(brand name)* tennis shoes?
Should we only love persons who take baths every day?
Should we only love persons who have lots of money?
Because God loves all persons, who should we love? *(Everyone!)*

Say: God's love is for all people—not just for some people, not just for the people we like or the people who are like us. Like Jonah, sometimes we have to learn to love people, and we may need God's help. Sometimes there are people who are hard to love. Think about those people now. We know God loves those people. God can help us love those people, too.

Pray: Dear God, sometimes there are people who are hard to love. But we know that you love those people, too. Help us to learn to love them. Amen.

**27**

**REPRODUCIBLE 2A**

ALL-IN-ONE BIBLE FUN

# Joshua

## Bible Verse

For God all things are possible.
Matthew 19:26

## Bible Story

Joshua 6

The story of the battle of Jericho is one that has been shared for many generations in word and in song. For a ragtag group of Israelites who had been wandering in the wilderness for forty years, this event served as definitive proof that God was with them and that the Promised Land was soon to become a reality.

Jericho stood at the entrance to the valley. In order for the Hebrew people to advance, this city had to fall. But it was a walled fortress, well protected. God's instructions were precise. For six days, Joshua and the soldiers of Israel were to march around the city of Jericho, blowing trumpets. The procession was to be led by the priests blowing rams' horns and the priests bearing the Ark of the Covenant. On the seventh day, after a long blast with the ram's horn, the people were to shout. Shout they did, just as God commanded. And the walls fell down flat. God delivered the city of Jericho into the hands of the Israelites.

The Bible is filled with wonderful stories that tell about God's actions throughout human history. All of these actions are beyond the accomplishment of mere human beings. God called a world into being. God created a great flood. God brought forth a series of plagues that finally freed God's people. God brought down the stone barricade that surrounded Jericho. God raised God's only son from the dead. With God all things are possible.

Children have no problem with miracles. Miracles happen around them every day. The sun comes up, chicks hatch from eggs, rainbows appear in the sky. Encourage the children to stand in awe of the wonders around them. When children ask "why" something or other happens and you truly do not understand, simply say, "I don't know. Isn't it wonderful that God planned such a wonderful world?" Truly, with God, there is nothing that is impossible.

# All things are possible for God.

If time is limited, we recommend those activities that are noted in **boldface**. Depending on your time and the number of children, you may be able to include more activities.

| ACTIVITY | TIME | SUPPLIES | |
|---|---|---|---|
| **Joshua's Horns** | **10 minutes** | **Reproducible 3A, crayons or felt-tip markers, safety scissors, tape** | JOIN THE FUN |
| Build a Wall | 15 minutes | paper grocery bags, newspaper, masking tape | |
| Nose and Toes | 5 minutes | None | BIBLE STORY FUN |
| Get Into Character | 5 minutes | paper horns (Reproducible 3A), Reproducible 3B, scissors | |
| **Bible Story: The Falling Walls** | **10 minutes** | **paper horns (Reproducible 3A), Reproducible 3B, scissors** | |
| Sing the Story | 5 minutes | paper horns (Reproducible 3A) | |
| Impossible Things | 10 minutes | yarn, scissors | LIVE THE FUN |
| **Possible Prayers** | **5 minutes** | **ball** | |

# Joshua's Horns

Greet the children as they arrive in the room. Involve them by letting them help you set out the materials for the first activity. Ask questions about their week and their family. Make this a time to touch base with your group.

Photocopy the pattern for Joshua's Horns **(Reproducible 3A)**. Give each child a pattern. Let them color the exterior and then cut it out. Show them how to roll and tape it to make a horn.

**Say: In today's Bible story, the horn plays a very important role. A man defeats a whole city with just the sound of a horn and the shout from the people. Does that sound impossible? Well, for ordinary people, it might be.**

### All things are possible for God.

Have the children place their horn in an out-of-the-way place until time for the story.

# Build a Wall

Set out paper grocery sacks and stacks of newspaper. Put the children in pairs.

**Say: We are going to build a wall. Since we don't have any stone, we are going to build our wall of newspaper and grocery sacks. When I say, "Go!" one person will get a grocery sack and the other will get newspaper. Wad the newspaper and stuff the grocery sacks. When the sack is filled, fold over the top and tape with masking tape. Bring your "stone" and place it here at the edge of the storytelling area. When one stone is finished, get another sack and some more newspaper and keep building. Let's see how high a wall we can build. Ready, set, go!**

Try to create a wall around the storytelling area using the sacks stacked on top of one another.

# Nose and Toes

Have the children stand inside the walls of Jericho. Play a game of "Joshua Says" (like "Simon Says") with the children.

Say: Joshua says, touch your knee. Joshua says, touch your ear. Joshua says, hop in place. Joshua says, touch the floor. Joshua says, run in place. Stop. Joshua says, stop.

Say: Those were pretty easy. Let's try again. Joshua says, jump up and down. Joshua says, stop. Joshua says, jump up and touch the ceiling. *(Let the children try to jump higher and higher.)* What's the matter? *(It's impossible to touch the ceiling simply by jumping.)*

Say: Joshua says, touch your nose to your toes. Joshua says, touch your nose to your finger. Joshua says, touch your nose to your elbow. What's the matter? *(It's impossible to touch your nose to your elbow.)*

Stop the game.

Say: Some things seem impossible for us to do. But today we'll hear a Bible story about a man who did the impossible, with a lot of help from God.

All things are possible for God.

# Get Into Character

Photocopy and cut apart the cue cards **(Reproducible 3B)**. Distribute paper horns **(Reproducible 3A)** to the children.

Say: I'm going to let you help me tell our Bible story today. Each of you will have a very important part. When I hold up the card that has that part on it, you will do the certain action that goes with that part.

Choose a single child or small group of children to do each activity, or let the whole group perform it at one time. Let the children practice each movement as you hold up a card.

**Hebrew people** — stand up and march in place, loudly.
**City of Jericho** — stand up and link arms.
**Joshua** — stand up and salute like a soldier.
**Priests** — make a trumpet sound into your paper horn.
Practice mixing up the cards and letting the children perform the action.

## Supplies

None

## Supplies

paper horns (Reproducible 3A), Reproducible 3B, scissors

**33**

# The Falling Walls

by LeeDell Stickler

> *While reading, hold up the cue card* **(Reproducible 3B)** *where the words are written in bold type. Pause to give the children the amount of time needed to perform the actions they learned in the "Get Into Character" activity. If the wall you built for the "Build a Wall" activity is large enough, bring the children inside the wall in order to tell the story.*

For forty years the **HEBREW PEOPLE** had wandered in the wilderness. They traveled here. They traveled there. They were beginning to get tired of traveling. Moses had grown very old. God had chosen **JOSHUA** to be the new leader.

God decided that the people were ready to go into the Promised Land. But entering the Promised Land wasn't so easy. At the head of the valley, the valley that led into the Promised Land, there stood a great city—the **CITY OF JERICHO**.

It was a large city with great high walls all around it to protect it. If the **HEBREW PEOPLE** wanted to enter the Promised Land, they had to get past the **CITY OF JERICHO**. But the people who lived in the city did not want the **HEBREW PEOPLE** to come into the Promised Land.

"Hmmmm," **JOSHUA** thought to himself. "The **CITY OF JERICHO** is surrounded by a great wall. It is too high to climb. It is too strong to knock down. The gates are tightly closed. It is impossible to capture this city."

But God said to **JOSHUA**, "I've got a plan. But you must follow it exactly as I tell you, even if it may seem strange to you."

"First you will march around the **CITY OF JERICHO** one time, with the soldiers, the priests, and the people. The **HEBREW PEOPLE** should not make a single sound. Do this every day for six days."

"On the seventh day," God told **JOSHUA**, "you will march around the **CITY OF JERICHO** seven times. As you march, the **PRIESTS** will blow their horns. At a special signal, the

ALL-IN-ONE BIBLE FUN

**PRIESTS** will make one long, loud blast on the horns. At that time I want all the **HEBREW PEOPLE** to shout as loud as they can. The walls of the **CITY OF JERICHO** will fall down."

So, **JOSHUA** told the **HEBREW PEOPLE** what God had told him to do. Even though it seemed impossible, the people decided, "We must do just as God said."

The **HEBREW PEOPLE** marched quietly around the city. *(Have the children get up and march around the paper bag wall. If you did not build a wall, have the children march in a circle.)*

The people from inside the **CITY OF JERICHO** looked out at the silent army. "What was going on?" they wondered. They yelled at the people and made fun of them.

For five more days the **HEBREW PEOPLE** marched silently around the **CITY OF JERICHO** and returned to their camp. *(March the children around the paper bag wall five more times.)*

Everyone was beginning to wonder what was going to happen.

On the seventh day, the **HEBREW PEOPLE** marched around the **CITY OF JERICHO** one time, two times, three times, four times, five times, six times, seven times, just as **JOSHUA** had told them. The **PRIESTS** blew the horns as they marched.

Then after the seventh time around the **PRIESTS** blew one loud, long blast on the horns. **JOSHUA** gave the signal. The **HEBREW PEOPLE** shouted. *(Have the children shout.)*

What a loud noise there was. Then, everyone watched as the walls of the **CITY OF JERICHO** began to crack and crumble and rumble and roar.

Just as God had promised, the walls of the **CITY OF JERICHO** fell down flat. *(Have the children knock the wall they built to the ground. If you did not build a wall, make arm motions to indicate falling down.)*

Heroes of the Bible - Elementary   Permission granted to photocopy for local church use. © 2007, 2010 Abingdon Press.

## Supplies

paper horns
(Reproducible
3A)

# Sing the Story

Have the children bring their paper horns **(Reproducible 3A)** to an open area of the room. Sing the following song to the tune of "Down by the Riverside" to sing the story of Joshua with the children.

**Say: We have heard the story of Joshua and the walls of Jericho. Now we're going to sing the story.**

> We're gonna march 'round the city walls,
> *(March in a circle.)*
> All 'round ol' Jericho,
> All 'round ol' Jericho,
> All 'round ol' Jericho,
> We're gonna march 'round the city walls,
> All 'round ol' Jericho,
> All 'round ol' Jericho.
>
> We're gonna blow on our trumpets there,
> *(Pretend to blow paper horns.)*
> All 'round ol' Jericho,
> All 'round ol' Jericho,
> All 'round ol' Jericho,
> We're gonna blow on our trumpets there,
> All 'round ol' Jericho,
> All 'round ol' Jericho.
>
> We're gonna shout out with a great shout,
> *(Stop marching, cup hands around mouth.)*
> All 'round ol' Jericho,
> All 'round ol' Jericho,
> All 'round ol' Jericho,
> We're gonna shout out with a great shout,
> All 'round ol' Jericho,
> All 'round ol' Jericho.
>
> We're gonna watch those walls come tumblin' down,
> *(Hold arms above head, bring hands down to touch the floor.)*
> All 'round ol' Jericho,
> All 'round ol' Jericho,
> All 'round ol' Jericho,
> We're gonna watch those walls come tumblin' down,
> All 'round ol' Jericho,
> All 'round ol' Jericho.

Based on Joshua 6
Words: Daphna Flegal
© 2001 Abingdon Press

# Impossible Things

**Supplies**

yarn, scissors

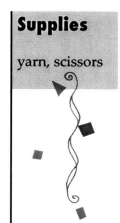

Give each child a 36-inch piece of yarn. Have each child tie the ends of the piece of yarn together to create a circle. Have the children place their circles on the floor and stand inside their circles.

Say: **I am going to make several statements. Some are possible. Some are impossible. Whenever I say something that is impossible, then everyone has to change circles. As you jump into a new circle, you have to say our Bible verse, "For God all things are possible" (Matthew 19:26). Each time I say something that is impossible, I will remove one of the yarn circles. More than one person can share a circle, but everyone has to have some part of his or her body inside a circle, even if it's only a foot or a finger.**

Use regular statements such as: I can read standing up. I can eat an ice cream cone in the car. I can swim in a lake. I can live without a television. I can sleep during the day. Bats can fly. Cats can climb trees. Seals can swim under water. God is always with me. Jesus loves me.

Mix in some of these impossible statements: Horses can fly. Trees grow up-side down. Waterfalls can fall up. Cows can give chocolate milk. People can stand on the sun. Hamburgers grow on trees. A fish can climb trees. A sheep can grow striped wool.

Mix the statements up to keep the children on their toes. After each impossible statement, remove one of the circles. Soon all the children will be standing with either a foot or a finger inside one circle.

# Possible Prayers

**Supplies**

ball

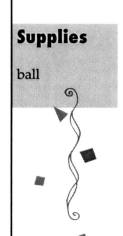

Bring the children together for a closing prayer.

Say: **Like Joshua, we can ask for God's help with problems that we think are impossible to solve.**

Hold the ball in your hands and **say: When I have a problem, I will remember** [Pause and wait for the children to respond with the Bible verse, "For God all things are possible" (Matthew 19:26).].

Toss the ball to another child, who will also **say: When I have a problem, I will remember** (Everyone says the Bible verse together.).

When every child has had a chance to say the verse out loud, close with a final prayer.

Pray: **Dear God, sometimes we have problems that seem impossible. Help us to remember that for you, all things are possible. Amen.**

**37**

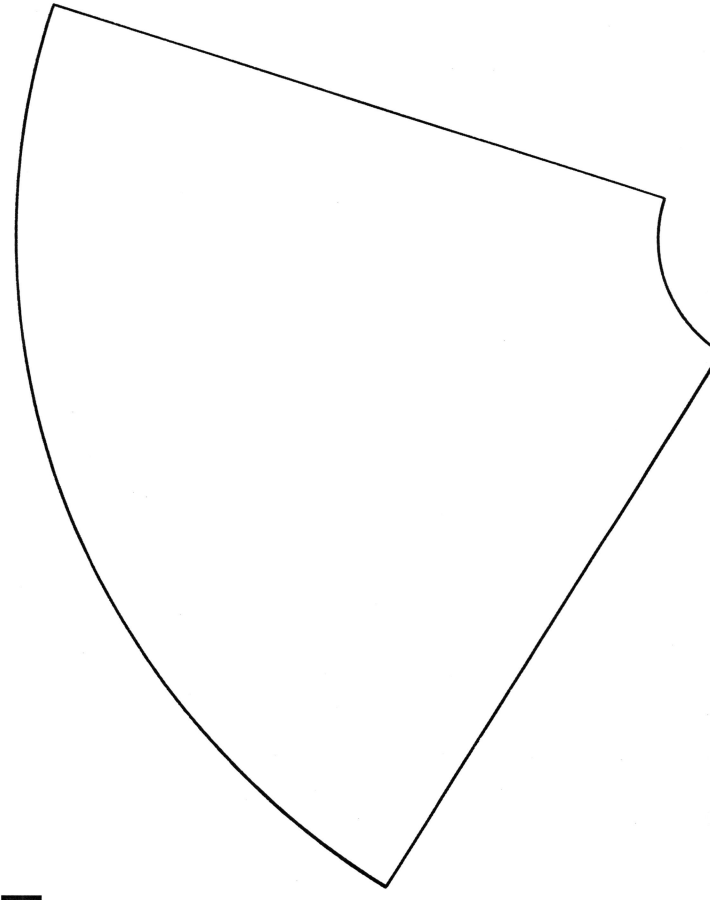

**REPRODUCIBLE 3A**

ALL-IN-ONE BIBLE FUN

# City of Jericho

# Joshua

# Priests

# Hebrew People

REPRODUCIBLE 3B

39

# Noah

## Bible Verse

I have set my bow in the clouds, and it shall be a sign of the covenant between me and the earth.

Genesis 9:13

## Bible Story

Genesis 6–9

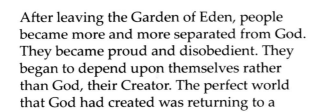
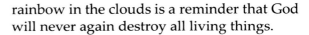

After leaving the Garden of Eden, people became more and more separated from God. They became proud and disobedient. They began to depend upon themselves rather than God, their Creator. The perfect world that God had created was returning to a state of chaos. So, God decided to try again.

In this new beginning, God would save a faithful few who would have a new chance to choose an obedient relationship with God and a relationship of love and respect with one another. Noah's faithfulness and obedience to God made him God's choice to be a part of the new beginning.

The Flood marked the end of the first era in the history of God's people. When the Flood was over, God promised Noah that even though sin would continue to exist, God would never again destroy humankind or curse the ground of the entire world. The

rainbow in the clouds is a reminder that God will never again destroy all living things.

A promise is a promise is a promise. Never make a promise to a child that you do not intend to keep. A child remembers a promise made by an adult and expects that adult to keep that promise. An adult that continually breaks promises to children soon loses credibility. Children will no longer trust that person. To teach children about God's promise, it is important to impress upon them the sacredness of a promise. The dependability of adult promises helps children understand better the promises of God.

However, we do need to help children understand that there are promises people should never make. A promise should never hurt anyone or allow a person to do something that might hurt them. God's promises are not like that.

# We can depend on God's promises.

If time is limited, we recommend those activities that are noted in **boldface**. Depending on your time and the number of children, you may be able to include more activities.

| ACTIVITY | TIME | SUPPLIES | |
|---|---|---|---|
| **What Am I?** | **10 minutes** | **Reproducible 4A, masking tape** | JOIN THE FUN |
| Animal Talk | 10 minutes | animal cards (Reproducible 4A) | |
| In the Ark | 10 minutes | animal cards (Reproducible 4A) | BIBLE STORY FUN |
| Rhyme Time | 5 minutes | None | |
| **Bible Story: Noah and the Big Boat** | **10 minutes** | **None** | |
| Keeping Promises | 5 minutes | Reproducible 4B, scissors | |
| Impossible Promises | 5 minutes | ball | LIVE THE FUN |
| **Rainbow Prayers** | **5 minutes** | **crayons, large piece of paper or newsprint for each child** | |

# What Am I?

Photocopy and cut apart the animal cards **(Reproducible 4A)**, making sure you have enough cards for each child to have one. Place the cards face down so they are convenient as the children arrive, but not visible.

Greet the children warmly as they come in. Without letting them see the animal, attach an animal card to their backs with masking tape.

**Say: What I am putting on your back is part of a game we will be playing when everyone arrives. Don't peek or ask your friends what is on your back.**

When everyone arrives, **say: You are to discover what animal is on your back. You cannot look in a mirror. You cannot ask a friend to tell you. What you can do is ask one or more friends questions that can be answered by a "yes" or a "no." For example, does the animal have legs? Does the animal have fur? When you think you have the identity of the animal on your back, come and whisper your guess to me. If you are right, then you can move the animal card from your back to your front and come to the storytelling area. If you are wrong, you must keep asking questions.**

Children who have a difficult time may be given strategic hints. As the children discover their animal, make sure the animals are taped securely to their front.

**Say: Today our Bible story includes lots of animals, a big boat, and a great flood. It is the story of Noah. From this story we learn something very important about God.**

## We can depend on God's promises.

# Animal Talk

Have the children sit in a circle on the floor. Identify the different animals **(Reproducible 4A)** the children have.

**Say: In our Bible story, God tells a man named Noah to build an ark, a very large boat. Then God told Noah to gather two of every kind of animal onto the ark. I wonder what that sounded like. When I say, "Go," I want you to make the sound of the animal on your picture. When I say, "stop," then everyone must stop.**

Say, "Go." Let the children continue to make animal noises for a couple of minutes. Then say, "stop."

# In the Ark

**Supplies**

animal cards (Reproducible 4A)

Have the children bring their chairs into a circle. Leave the middle large and open. Select one child to be Noah. Remove that child's chair from the circle.

Say: In our Bible story, God tells a man named Noah to build an ark. Then God told Noah to gather two of every kind of animal onto the ark. From this story we learn something important.

> **We can depend on God's promises.**

Choose a child to be Noah. Have Noah stand in the middle of the circle.

Say: Noah will call out the name of an animal pictured on our animal cards. Noah will name one animal at a time. The child (or children) with that animal card must go into the "ark" (center of the circle) beside Noah. Sometimes, Noah will call, "Everybody out!" Then all the animals that are in the center of the circle must find a new seat. Noah will try to get one of the empty seats. The person left without a seat becomes Noah. Noah may call to the ark as many or as few animals as he or she chooses before saying, "Everybody out!"

# Rhyme Time

**Supplies**

None

Sing the song "On Noah's Ark" to the tune of "Down by the Bay." Encourage the children to make up additional rhymes.

On Noah's ark
All the animals stay;
Down in the dark
Is where they play.
And if you look,
Old Noah will say,
"Did you ever see a bear
With curly hair
On Noah's ark?"

On Noah's ark
All the animals stay;
Down in the dark
Is where they play.
And if you look,
Old Noah will say,

"Did you ever see a pig
Dancing a jig
On Noah's ark?"

On Noah's ark
All the animals stay;
Down in the dark
Is where they play.
And if you look,
Old Noah will say,
"Did you ever see a snail
Chasing its tail
On Noah's ark?"

Word: Daphna and Gary Flegal
© 2001 Abingdon Press

# Noah and the Big Boat

by LeeDell Stickler

**Say:** You are going to help tell this story today. Between each section of the story is a little poem. The poem has motions. We'll do the motions together.

**Refrain:**
**1. Drip, drop, pitter, patter.**
*(Pinch fingers of right hand together, touch left palm. Then repeat motion with left hand. Do this twice.)*

**2. Raindrops fill the air.**
*(Hold hands above head, wiggle fingers as though rain falling as you lower hands.)*

**3. Even though the thunder rolls,**
*(Close hands. Arms are bent at elbow. Make circles by rolling arms around one another.)*

**4. God's love will still be there.**
*(Cross arms over chest. Extend arms out in front, palms up.)*

When God looked down upon the
   earth
And saw the evil there,
God thought the time had surely
   come
To start again down there.
God looked at all the people
Doing things that they should not.
God looked for someone faithful,
Some bright and shining spot.
It was then that God found Noah.
A faithful man and true,
Noah and his family lived
As God had told them to.

**Refrain:**

Noah, I'm not happy
With things the way they are.
I want to start all over,

So you must build an ark.
Make it big and sturdy,
I'll tell you just what size.
For two of every creature,
Must be housed inside.
So, Noah sawed and hammered
A boat of cypress wood.
He gathered all the animals in,
As God told him he should.

There were elephants and ocelots,
Giraffes and kangaroos,
Lions, tigers, and polar bears,
They came in two by two.
There were antelopes and cheetahs,
Ring-tailed cats and camels, too.
There were slinky snakes and turtles,
In Noah's floating zoo.
When two of every kind were there,
God closed them all in tight.

ALL-IN-ONE BIBLE FUN

And soon the rain began to fall
For forty days and nights.

**Refrain.**

Splitter, splatter, dripety, drop,
The rain fell on the boat.
Creak, crack, crickety, crunch,
The boat began to float.
The rain continued falling.
It covered up the land.
Soon there was nothing left to see.
But Noah's little band.
The ark rode on the water.
It floated to and fro.
It had no destination;
There was no place to go.

One day the rain did cease to fall.
The wind began to blow.
The waters that had filled the earth
Soon began to go.
The ark came to a resting place
Atop a mountain high.
So, through the open window,
Noah let a dove go fly.
"Fly around my little dove,
The sky is turning fair."
But soon the little dove returned
No place to land out there.

So, Noah waited patiently,
Then sent the dove back out.
What she brought back to the boat
Made Noah jump and shout.
She carried in her tiny beak,
A sign that there was spring.

The water-covered earth below,
Now had some growing things.
So, Noah sent her out again
To look both east and west.
This time the dove did not return.
She'd found a place to nest.

**Refrain.**

Noah opened up the door,
The animals rushed outside.
What a sound these creatures
                made—
Stompety, clompety, flutter, slide.
Then Noah built an altar
Upon the muddy ground.
"We thank you, God, most truly,
For keeping us safe and sound.
We thank you for giving us
A chance to start anew.
We'll try to live a better life
And do what we should do."

Then God spoke to Noah,
"Here's a promise to you from me.
I set my bow up in the clouds,
So you can clearly see.
I never will destroy the earth,
There'll always be a time,
Of planting and of harvesting,
On this world of mine.
My rainbow will remind you
Of the promise that we share,
That even though the thunder rolls,
My love will still be there."

**Refrain.**

**45**

# Keeping Promises

Photocopy and cut apart the picture cards **(Reproducible 4B)**. Give one to each child. If you have more than twelve children, make more than one copy or let them share.

**Say:** God made a promise to Noah. God promised never to destroy the earth again. God has kept the promise. We call this special promise a covenant.

> ## We can depend on God's promises.

**Ask:** What kind of promises do you make? Do you keep them? *(Invite the children to share the promises they have made recently.)* **What happens if you don't keep your promise?** *(You get into trouble. People don't trust you anymore.)*

**Say:** I am going to tell you about a promise someone made. You have the picture card that lets you know whether this person kept the promise or not. When you recognize your card, hold the card up. If the person kept the promise, stand up and shout, "Hurray!"

1. Eric promised to do his homework before he went outside to play.
2. Lisa promised to say her prayers before she went to bed.
3. Tommy promised to eat his dinner before he ate his dessert.
4. T.J. promised not to play in the vacant lot.
5. Liz promised to help her mother clean house.
6. Ellen promised to play with her little sister.
7. Danny promised to play with his little brother.
8. Jeff's dad promised to take him to the ball game.
9. Maya promised never to climb trees again.
10. Sheila promised to clean up her mess after making cookies.
11. Stephen promised not to watch television until he had finished his homework.
12. Alisa promised to take her time with her writing assignment.

**Ask:** What happens when you make a promise and don't keep it?

# Impossible Promises

Gather the children into a circle, either standing up or sitting on the floor. Talk about rainbows—the shape, the colors.

**Ask: Has God kept the promise?**

**Say: The rainbow reminds us that God will always keep the promise. A promise is very special. We should always try to keep our promises.**

**Ask: What happens when someone makes a promise to you and then doesn't keep it?** *(You stop believing that person.)* **Have you ever heard a person make a promise he or she couldn't possibly keep?** *(Invite the children to share promises that are impossible.)*

**Say: Let's make some impossible promises as we toss the ball. When you get the ball, you will make an impossible promise. I will begin. I promise that I will give each of you one million dollars for your birthday!**

Toss the ball to someone in the group. Continue until everyone has had a turn.

**Say: We know these promises are just for fun and that we cannot possibly keep them. But God made Noah a real promise. We can depend on God to keep that promise.**

**Supplies**

ball

# Rainbow Prayers

Give each child a large piece of paper or newsprint. Instruct the children to sit down in a cross-legged position so that their knees are slightly over one edge of the paper. Give each child three different colored crayons.

**Say: The rainbow is God's promise to never again destroy the earth.**

Have the children choose one of their crayons and draw an arch on their papers around their knees. This will make an rainbow shape.

**Say: The rainbow is God's promise that there will always be spring and summer, winter, and fall.**

Have each child choose a second crayon to draw another arch on the paper.

**Say: The rainbow is God's promise that God's love is always there.**

Have each child choose a third crayon to draw a third arch on the paper.

**Pray: Dear God, thank you for all your promises. Amen.**

**Supplies**

crayons, large piece of paper or newsprint for each child

**47**

**REPRODUCIBLE 4A**

ALL-IN-ONE BIBLE FUN

# David

## Bible Verse

If God is for us, who is against us?

Romans 8:31

## Bible Story

1 Samuel 17

King David was the most beloved of all the kings of Israel. Not only was he a great leader, but he was also a statesman and a shrewd politician. Because of David, Israel grew from a loose tribal confederacy into a strong nation. But how did it all happen? How did David, the ninth son of Jesse, a shepherd and a harp player, go from being a relative unknown to becoming King David, the royal champion of God?

David, even as a boy, was charming and charismatic. The stories about him that we find in the books of Samuel are similar to those that gather around any great national hero (like George Washington or Abraham Lincoln, for instance). The story the children will hear today is one of the more famous stories about David.

The Philistines were a warlike tribe of people who lived along the southern coast of Palestine. Superior in weapons, the Philistines were a constant threat to neighboring countries. The battle between Goliath (a

Philistine warrior) and David led to the defeat of the Philistines. David's victory also led to Saul's jealousy and the rift between him and David.

David was just a simple shepherd boy, the youngest of nine brothers. In the family, he was relatively unimportant. But in spite of his age and his inexperience, God had an important job for him to do. Your children can identify with David. Because of their age, they are often overlooked as being unimportant. But they are important to God. They have an important part to play in God's church. And with God's help, they can do important things.

# With God's help we can do important things.

If time is limited, we recommend those activities that are noted in **boldface**. Depending on your time and the number of children, you may be able to include more activities.

| ACTIVITY | TIME | SUPPLIES | |
|---|---|---|---|
| **Design a Shield** | **10 minutes** | **Reproducibles 5A and 5B, crayons or felt-tip markers, wooden craft sticks, tape or glue, scissors** | JOIN THE FUN |
| Balancing Act | 10 minutes | masking tape, chair, foam balls or paper crumpled into balls | |
| I Think I Can | 5 minutes | None | BIBLE STORY FUN |
| Let's Get Organized | 5 minutes | index cards (two sets) beginning with 1 and going up to the number of children participating | |
| **Bible Story: David and Goliath** | **10 minutes** | **Reproducible 5B** | |
| How Big Was Goliath? | 5 minutes | newspaper, masking tape, felt-tip markers, ruler | |
| Big Enough | 10 minutes | ten rocks, permanent marker, box or plastic tub | |
| Identify Goliaths | 10 minutes | trash can, chair, plain paper; masking tape, crayons or felt-tip markers | LIVE THE FUN |
| **Help Me, God** | **5 minutes** | **trash can from "Identify Goliaths," newspaper** | |

# JOIN THE FUN

## Supplies

Reproducibles 5A and 5B, crayons or felt-tip markers, wooden craft sticks, tape or glue, scissors

## Supplies

masking tape, chair, foam balls or paper crumpled into balls

# Design a Shield

Before class begins, photocopy the characters **(Reproducible 5B)** from today's Bible story. Children who arrive early may color the characters. Tape each character to a wooden craft stick for use in telling the Bible story later in the lesson.

Greet the children as they arrive. Give each child an undecorated shield **(Reproducible 5A)**. Let the children make their own designs for them.

Say: **A shield usually said something about the person who carried it. Our shield will say: "God is my shield." In today's Bible story, a boy fights a giant warrior. Instead of wearing armor and carrying a shield, the boy used God as his shield.**

Ask: **What do you think that means?**

# Balancing Act

Use the masking tape to designate a starting point. Have the children form a line behind the starting point. Place a chair about ten feet from the starting point. The children will face the chair. Give the first child a foam or paper ball.

Say: **When I say, "Go!" place the ball on the back of your hand and walk around the chair and back to the line. Then pass the ball to the next person in line. If the ball falls off, pick it up and put it back on. But that is the only time you may touch the ball with your hands. The object of the game is for everyone to go around the chair before I say, "Stop!"**

Make sure all the children are standing in line. Place the ball on the hand of the first child. Say, "Go!" and begin the game. Allow an adequate amount of time for the children to finish. After the game, pick up the ball(s) and put them away.

Ask: **Was the game fun to play? Was it easy or hard?** *(hard)* **What made it hard?** *(having to use the back of hands)* **What might have made it easier?** *(using hands palm up instead)* **Would that have been as much fun?**

Note for the Teacher: If you have a large class (more than ten children), use more than one ball. Don't try to set up competition between teams. The idea is for everyone to participate and have fun.

# I Think I Can

**Say: Think about all the things you do during a day. Some are easy. Some are hard. I am going to name some things. If you think they are easy to do, clap your hands very hard. If you think they are hard to do, stomp your feet on the floor. Let's practice. If they are easy**—*(let the children clap their hands)*, **if they are hard**—*(let the children stomp their feet)*.

Suggest these activities: brush your teeth, clean up your room, get dressed, brush your hair, take out the garbage, feed your pet, wash dishes, read a book, do math problems, spell words, play the piano, play soccer, ride a bicycle. (Make the list as long or as short as your time allows.)

**Say: Some jobs are hard for some people and easy for others. In today's Bible story, we will hear about a young boy whose brothers thought he was too young, too small, and too weak to do something important. But he didn't let their feelings stop him. He knew God would help him.**

## With God's help we can do important things.

# Let's Get Organized!

Have the children arrange themselves in order from the shortest to the tallest. Then give each child a number, designating his or her place in the line. Have them hold the numbers in their right hands. Number one will be the tallest child.

**Ask: How does it feel to be small? What would you do differently if you were taller? How does it feel to be tall? What would you do differently if you were smaller?**

Then have the children arrange themselves according to their age. You may want to have a calendar in the room to make this a little easier. Then give out the second set of numbers. Have them hold these numbers in their left hands. Number one will be the oldest child.

**Ask: Which number is higher, the one in your right hand or the one in your left hand? Just because you are taller, does that mean you are older? Just because you are older, does that mean you are taller?**

**Say: In our Bible story today a boy named David learns an important lesson. It doesn't make any difference what size you are or how old you are. With God's help you can do important things.**

**53**

# David and Goliath

by LeeDell Stickler

---

**Ask: How many of you have older brothers or sisters? Do they ever tease you because you are younger than they are? Do they ever get to do things that you do not? How does this make you feel? Are there things you can do that they can not?**

**Say: In this Bible story, a younger brother has this problem. But he learns that with God's help he can do almost anything.**

Hand out the story figures **(Reproducible 5B)** to several children.

**Say: Those of you with story figures, come up to the front. Whenever you hear the name of your character, I want you to hold it up.**

Introduce the characters: David, David's brothers, Jesse, David's father, sheep, King Saul, soldier, Goliath.

---

A man named Jesse *(Hold up Jesse figure.)* had eight sons. David *(Hold up David figure.)* was the youngest. Each of his brothers was older, bigger, and stronger than David.

"You are too young," said one. "You are too small," said another. The brothers were really thinking, "You are not very important."

But David knew better. *(Hold up David figure.)* "I may be little, but with God's help I can do important things."

David cared for his family's sheep. *(Hold up sheep figure.)* He helped the sheep find green grass and cool water. He used his sling to protect his flock from lions and bears.

David often prayed, "Thank you, God, for helping me be a good shepherd." And David said to himself, "I may be little, but with God's help I can do important things."

One day his father called him in from the field. *(Hold up Jesse figure.)* "David, I have a job for you to do. Take some food to your brothers who are soldiers in King Saul's army. Bring back news of how they are," said his father.

David traveled to where King Saul's army was in the valley. *(Hold up King Saul figure.)* He also saw another army on the hillside. Both armies were ready for battle. David hurriedly found his brothers. *(Hold up three brothers figure.)*

**54**

Just then a soldier stepped from the ranks of the other army. (*Hold up Goliath figure.*) He was big—bigger than any man David had ever seen. The soldier yelled, "My name is Goliath! Choose a man to fight me. Whoever wins this fight, wins the war." No one came forward. Everyone was afraid of Goliath.

"Why doesn't someone go forward and fight him?" asked David. (*Hold up David figure.*)

"Why do you care?" his brothers asked. (*Hold up three brothers figure.*) "You're too young to fight."

"I may be young," said David. "But with God's help I can do almost anything." (*Hold up David figure.*)

A soldier (*Hold up soldier figure.*) took David (*Hold up David figure.*) to King Saul. (*Hold up King Saul figure.*) He told the king what David had said. King Saul shook his head. "You cannot fight this soldier. You are too young," said the king.

But David (*Hold up David figure.*) said, "Since I was a young boy, I have cared for my father's sheep. I have killed a lion and a bear who attacked my sheep with just my sling. God, who saved me from the lion and the bear, will save me from Goliath."

So King Saul (*Hold up King Saul figure.*) gave David (*Hold up David figure.*) his helmet, his armor, and his sword. But they were so heavy that David could hardly walk. "I will fight this man with just my sling," said David.

So, David found five smooth stones and went out to fight Goliath. When Goliath (*Hold up Goliath figure.*) saw David coming, he began to laugh. "You are too little. I will make bird food of you!" Goliath shouted.

"I may be little. But with God's help I can do important things," David said to himself. (*Hold up David figure.*) Aloud David said, "You may have a sword and shield, but I stand here in the name of God." Then David placed a stone in the pocket of his sling. He swung the sling over his head, around and around and around. Then, he let it go. The stone flew through the air and struck Goliath on the forehead. Goliath fell to the ground. (*Drop Goliath figure.*)

Everyone was surprised, except David. (*Hold up David figure.*) "I may be young, I may be little, I may be weak. But with God's help I can do important things."

newspaper, masking tape, felt-tip markers, ruler

# How Big Was Goliath?

Tape sheets of newspaper together until they measure about nine feet in length. Tape this to the wall.

**Say: The Bible tells us that Goliath was nine feet tall. Let's see how tall you are next to Goliath.**

Have the children stand up next to the newspaper, put a mark at the place where their heads reach and then write their names beside the mark. Have them step back to see how much taller Goliath was than they are.

**Ask: How do you think the soldiers felt when they saw the nine feet tall giant? How did David's brothers feel? Do you think they trembled? Let's tremble. Do you think they hid? Let's hide. Do you think they ran away? Let's run away!**

Bring the children back together.

**Ask: How do you think David felt?**

Supplies

ten rocks, permanent marker, box or plastic tub

# Big Enough

Use a permanent marker to write each word of the Bible verse and the Scripture reference on a rock: "If God is for us, who is against us?" (Romans 8:31). Try to locate rocks that are large enough that, when carried together, are pretty heavy. Place the rocks in a box or plastic tub.

**Say: David knew that he was big enough to fight Goliath. He knew that with God's help he could do important things. Let's see if you are big enough to handle something heavy.**

Have the children sit or stand in a circle and pass the container of rocks around the circle one time. Then have the children pass it around a second time, with each child removing one rock from the container. Have the children lay the rocks on the floor or on a table to form the Bible verse. Invite the children to repeat the Bible verse together.

Next, pass the container around as the children repeat the Bible verse. Have each child add one rock at a time back to the container.

> **With God's help we can do important things.**

# Identify Goliaths

Say: We may not have to fight giants, but we have problems that are difficult for us to fight. We may not be very good at reading, we may be scared of the dark, we may be afraid of spiders or snakes, we may have a bully at school who makes us feel uncomfortable, or we may have parents who are going through a divorce. God can help us overcome all of these things.

Invite the children to think about a problem that they might have. Give each child a piece of plain paper. Encourage the children to either write the problem or draw a picture that shows the problem.

If the children are willing, let the children share what they have written or drawn.

Turn an empty trash can upside down on a chair. Move the chair and trash can in the middle of an open area. Help the children tape their papers all over the trash can.

**Supplies**

trash can, chair, plain paper; masking tape, crayons or felt-tip markers

# Help Me, God!

Have the children gather around the trash can.

Ask: What did we learn today from the story of David and Goliath? *(God can help us when we have difficult jobs to do.)*

Say: Look at all these hard things we have to do. Think about those hard things as we pray today. Picture God being with you as you do these hard things. Today, when we pray, we can say, "Help me, God!"

Pray: Dear God, sometimes we have problems we need help with. We know that with you, anything is possible. Here are some of our problems. *(Invite the children to share their problems with God verbally or silently.)* Help us. Amen.

Then give each child several sheets of newspaper. Have the children wad up the newspaper into small balls. Have the children throw the newspaper balls at the trash can. As they throw the balls have them say aloud, "I may be young, but with God's help I can do important things!"

Say: Just as God helped David defeat Goliath, God will help us face all the important tasks we have. Have the children pick up the newspaper balls when the activity is over.

**Supplies**

trash can from "Identify Goliaths," newspaper

**57**

**REPRODUCIBLE 5A**

Permission granted to photocopy for local church use. © 2007, 2010 Abingdon Press.     ALL-IN-ONE BIBLE FUN

David

Jesse

King Saul

sheep

soldier

David's brothers

Goliath

# Miriam and Moses

## Bible Verse

Love one another as I have loved you.

John 15:12

## Bible Story

Exodus 1:8–2:10

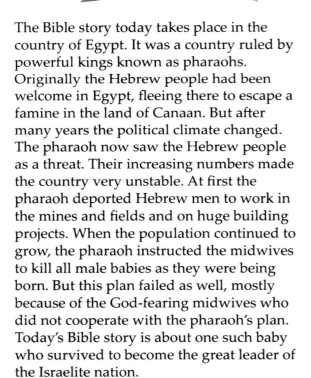

The Bible story today takes place in the country of Egypt. It was a country ruled by powerful kings known as pharaohs. Originally the Hebrew people had been welcome in Egypt, fleeing there to escape a famine in the land of Canaan. But after many years the political climate changed. The pharaoh now saw the Hebrew people as a threat. Their increasing numbers made the country very unstable. At first the pharaoh deported Hebrew men to work in the mines and fields and on huge building projects. When the population continued to grow, the pharaoh instructed the midwives to kill all male babies as they were being born. But this plan failed as well, mostly because of the God-fearing midwives who did not cooperate with the pharaoh's plan. Today's Bible story is about one such baby who survived to become the great leader of the Israelite nation.

The story of the Exodus is the one event that turned the Hebrew people into the Israelite nation. Moses played a pivotal role in this story, but it was courageous women who made it possible for Moses to live and fulfill his destiny.

God planned for families to provide for the emotional and physical needs of children. However, in today's world, more than fifty percent of marriages end in divorce. We cannot change the modern situation, but we can encourage family members to love and support one another.

As a teacher, it is important for you to be affirming and keep yourself informed about what is happening in your children's lives. Children need to know that there are significant adults who care for them and provide for them. It is through the love and care of families that children learn more about God's love and care. At times when families are torn apart, it is important for the church to be the extended family where children can find the love they need.

# We can show love to family members.

If time is limited, we recommend those activities that are noted in **boldface**. Depending on your time and the number of children, you may be able to include more activities.

| ACTIVITY | TIME | SUPPLIES | |
|---|---|---|---|
| **Watch It!** | 10 minutes | cloth or construction paper; items found in the room such as a box of crayons, glue, scissors, a Bible, and a marker | JOIN THE FUN |
| Search for Moses | 5 minutes | Reproducible 6A, scissors, tape or glue | BIBLE STORY FUN |
| **Get Into Character** | **5 minutes** | **None** | |
| **Bible Story: Miriam and Moses** | **10 minutes** | **baby in the basket (Reproducible 6A)** | |
| Hide the Baby | 10 minutes | baby in the basket (Reproducible 6A) | |
| Sing the Story | 5 minutes | None | |
| Basket Full of Love | 10 minutes | Reproducible 6B, scissors, crayons or colored pencils, glue or stapler and staples | LIVE THE FUN |
| **Bless the Families** | **5 minutes** | **baby in the basket (Reproducible 6A)** | |

# Join the Fun

## Supplies

cloth or construction paper; items found in the room such as a box of crayons, glue, scissors, a Bible, and a marker

# Watch It!

Greet the children as they arrive. Try to say something personal to each child. Remember these are God's children. God loves each and every one of them.

Have the children sit in a circle on the floor.

**Ask: How many of you have ever been asked to keep watch over something or someone while your parent or another adult had to leave the room for a minute?** (*Invite the children to share their experiences.*) **Why do you think they wanted you to watch this person or thing?** (*for protection, to keep anything bad from happening*)

**Say: Today we are going to see what kind of watchers you are.**

Have the children gather around three sides of a table. Place several items on the table. (Use objects from the room.)

**Say: Look very carefully at each object. Then close your eyes. I will remove one or more objects. When you open your eyes, try to remember which objects are missing.**

Give the children a moment to look at all the items on the table. Then have the children close their eyes and turn so that they're facing away from the items. Cover the items with a cloth or piece of construction paper while you remove one or two objects.

Have the children turn back around. Remove the cloth or paper. Have the children try to identify which object or objects are missing.

Do this several times. As the children get more and more accustomed to the items on the table, begin to remove more than one.

**Say: In today's Bible story, we hear about members of a special family. These family members loved and cared for one another just like your family members love and care for you. One of the family members cared for her little brother by watching over him.**

> # We can show love to family members.

# Search for Moses

Reproducible 6A, scissors, tape or glue

Before class begins, photocopy, cut out, and assemble the reed basket and baby Moses **(Reproducible 6A)**. Place Moses (rolled into a tube shape) in the basket and secure the lid. Then hide the baby and basket somewhere in the room. Make sure it is visible but not very obvious.

**Ask: Have you ever been asked to take care of a younger brother or sister or other member of your family? How did you feel when you were asked to do this? How did you feel while you were doing this? Who watches over you? What do they do to show you that they love and care for you?** *(Suggest things such as: providing food, providing care during illness, providing clothing, providing love, and so forth.)*

**Say: Watching over a brother or sister is one way families show love for one another.**

## We can show love to family members.

**Say: In today's Bible story, we learn about a baby who is hidden by his family to protect him. Somewhere in this room Jochebed [JOK uh bed] has hidden baby Moses in his basket. I want you to pretend to be baby Moses' brother or sister. It is your job to keep a watch over him. Walk around the room. When you see the baby, don't tell anyone else. Just clap your hands and say, "Baby in a basket. I'm watching you." Then come to the story circle. Practice the phrase several times.**

Allow the children time to locate the baby and move to the story circle.

# Get Into Character

None

**Say: I want you to help me tell the Bible story today. But you have to listen very carefully. Every time you hear certain names, I want you to do certain actions. When you hear the word king, stomp your feet three times.** *(Let the children practice.)* **When you hear the name** *Jochebed* **[JOK-uh-bed], rock your baby.** *(Let the children practice.)* **When you hear the name** *Miriam,* **hold your hands up in front of your face with your fingers spread as through you are looking through the grass.** *(Let the children practice.)* **When you hear the word** *princess* **pat your hair as though you are admiring yourself.** *(Let the children practice.)*

Say the names several times to let the children practice.

# Miriam and Moses

by LeeDell Stickler

---

Pass the Baby Moses **(Reproducible 6A)** around the circle. Make comments such as: What a strange bed. There's even a lid on it. I wonder why.

**Say: Because of a loving family, this tiny** baby grew up. And when he grew up, God had a special plan for him. He became the one who led his people out of slavery in Egypt and into the Promised Land. But you will hear that story at a different time.

---

During a time of famine, the Hebrew people left their home and came to Egypt to live. Over the years their numbers grew and grew.

Then one day a new **king** (*Stomp three times.*) came to the throne. He did not like the Hebrews. So the **king** (*Stomp three times.*) made the Hebrew people into slaves.

The Hebrew people worked very hard cutting stone and making bricks to build new cities for the **king**. (*Stomp three times.*) But their numbers still grew. This did not make the **king** (*Stomp three times.*) happy. He decided to kill all Hebrew baby boys that were born.

One day a baby boy was born into a Hebrew family. "We must hide the baby to keep him safe," said his mother, **Jochebed**. (*Rock the baby.*)

So, **Jochebed** (*Rock the baby.*) went to the river and collected armfuls of brown reeds. She wove these reeds into a basket that was just the size of her baby. She also wove a lid for the basket. When the basket and lid were finished, she painted the outside with pitch. Pitch would keep the basket watertight.

**Jochebed** (*Rock the baby.*) lined the basket with soft blankets. Then she placed her baby inside and put the lid on.

"Come with me, **Miriam**," (*Peek through the grasses.*) said **Jochebed** (*Rock the baby.*) to her daughter. They carried the basket to the river's edge. **Jochebed** (*Rock the baby.*) put the basket into the water among the reeds. Because the basket was made of reeds, **Miriam** (*Peek through the grasses.*) could hardly see it.

"**Miriam**, (*Peek through the grasses.*) you must watch over your brother," **Jochebed** (*Rock the baby.*) said.

ALL-IN-ONE BIBLE FUN

**Jochebed** *(Rock the baby.)* did not want to leave her baby in the river, but it was the only way to keep him safe. That was how **Jochebed** *(Rock the baby.)* showed her love for her baby son.

So, **Miriam** *(Peek through the grasses.)* hid in the tall river grasses and watched. It was her special job to take care of her brother. That was how **Miriam** *(Peek through the grasses.)* showed her love for him.

**Miriam** *(Peek through the grasses.)* kept watching. Suddenly she heard voices. She peered through the reeds. It was the **king's** *(Stomp three times.)* daughter and her servants. The **princess** *(Pat hair.)* had come to take a bath!

As the **princess** *(Pat hair.)* waded into the water, she saw the basket. "Whatever is that basket doing there?" she asked. "Bring it to me."

A serving girl waded into the water to the basket. Then she bought it to the **princess**. *(Pat hair.)*

The **princess** *(Pat hair.)* lifted the lid off the basket. "Oh," she cooed, "what a beautiful baby! Some Hebrew mother has hidden her child here on the river to keep him safe. I cannot let my father, the **king**,

*(Stomp three times.)* harm this baby. I will take him home and raise him as my own!"

**Miriam** *(Peek through the grasses.)* was frightened. What would happen to her little brother? Just then she had an idea. She jumped up from her hiding place and ran to the **princess**. *(Pat hair.)* "Shall I get someone to help you care for this baby?"

The **princess** *(Pat hair.)* smiled. "I will need someone. Do you have anyone in mind?" **Miriam** *(Peek through the grasses.)* smiled and nodded. Then she began to run as fast as she could to her house.

"Mother, Mother, come quickly. The **king's** *(Stomp three times.)* daughter has found our baby! She wants to raise him as her own. She needs your help!" The two ran back to the river.

The **princess** *(Pat hair.)* handed the baby to **Jochebed**. *(Rock the baby.)* "I will pay you to care for this baby. When he is older, bring him to the palace to me."

**Jochebed** *(Rock the baby.)* cuddled her son close. Now she didn't have to hide her baby. And when he was older, she brought him to the palace where he grew to be a man.

**Supplies**

baby in the basket (Reproducible 6A)

# Hide the Baby

**Ask:** Why did Jochebed have to keep her baby a secret? Do you think it is easy to hide a baby? Why or why not? How did she hide him? How do you think Jochebed felt when she placed her baby in the river? Who kept watch over him? What happened?

**Say:** Now we are going to pretend that we are the princess who has come to the river to take a bath. She hears a baby cry and is trying to find it.

Select one child to be IT. IT will close his or her eyes as the teacher hides the baby again. When baby Moses is hidden, let IT open his or her eyes. The object is for IT to find baby Moses using the hints the class provides. The class provides the hints by crying like a baby. The closer IT comes to the baby, the louder the class members cry. The farther away IT moves from the baby, the softer the class members cry. When IT finds the baby, then IT selects the next child to be IT.

**Supplies**

None

# Sing the Story

**Say:** Baby Moses' family loved and cared for him. They kept him safe from the king. Let's name some ways we can show love to our family.

Encourage the children to name ways they can show love such as helping at home, watching younger brothers or sisters, saying "I love you," playing games with their family, praying for their family, and so forth.

Sing the following words to the tune of "Down by the Riverside."

### Down by the River Nile

His mother made him a basket boat,
Down by the river Nile,
Down by the river Nile,
Down by the river Nile.
His mother made him a basket boat,
Down by the river Nile.

His mother put him inside the boat,
Down by the river Nile,
Down by the river Nile,
Down by the river Nile.
His mother put him inside the boat,
Down by the river Nile.

His sister watched him through the reeds,
Down by the river Nile,

Down by the river Nile,
Down by the river Nile.
His sister watched him through the reeds,
Down by the river Nile.

The princess found him inside the boat,
Down by the river Nile,
Down by the river Nile,
Down by the river Nile.
The princess found him inside the boat,
Down by the river Nile.

words: Daphna Flegal
Words © 2001 Abingdon Press

# Basket Full of Love

Photocopy the basket, handle, and coupons **(Reproducible 6B)** for each child.

**Say: Our families are very special. God wants us to show love to our families. We can do that in many different ways. Today we can make a "Basket Full of Love" to share.**

## We can show love to family members.

Have the children cut out the basket, handle, and coupons. Let the children decorate the cut-outs with crayons or colored pencils.

Show the children how to fold the basket on the dotted line. Then have the children glue or staple the two sides together. Help each child glue one end of the handle to the back and one end to the front. Place the coupons in the basket.

Read the coupons to the children. The coupons indicate the different ways the child agrees to show love to family members during the coming week.

# Bless the Families

Have the children sit in a circle. Show the children the baby in the basket **(Reproducible 6A)**.

**Say: Jochebed showed love to baby Moses when she hid him from the king. His sister showed love when she watched him floating in the river. The princess showed love when she adopted him. There are many ways we can show love to our families. Praying for our families is one important way we can show love. I will walk around behind you and give baby Moses in his basket to one of you. Then the whole class will say: Thank you God for (child's name) and for (child's name)'s family.**

Walk around the back of the circle and place the basket in one child's lap. Continue until every child has been included.

**Say: God is like a special family member. God loves and cares about us just as your family loves and cares for you.**

## Supplies

Reproducible 6B, scissors, crayons or colored pencils, glue or stapler and staples

## Supplies

baby in the basket (Reproducible 6A)

**67**

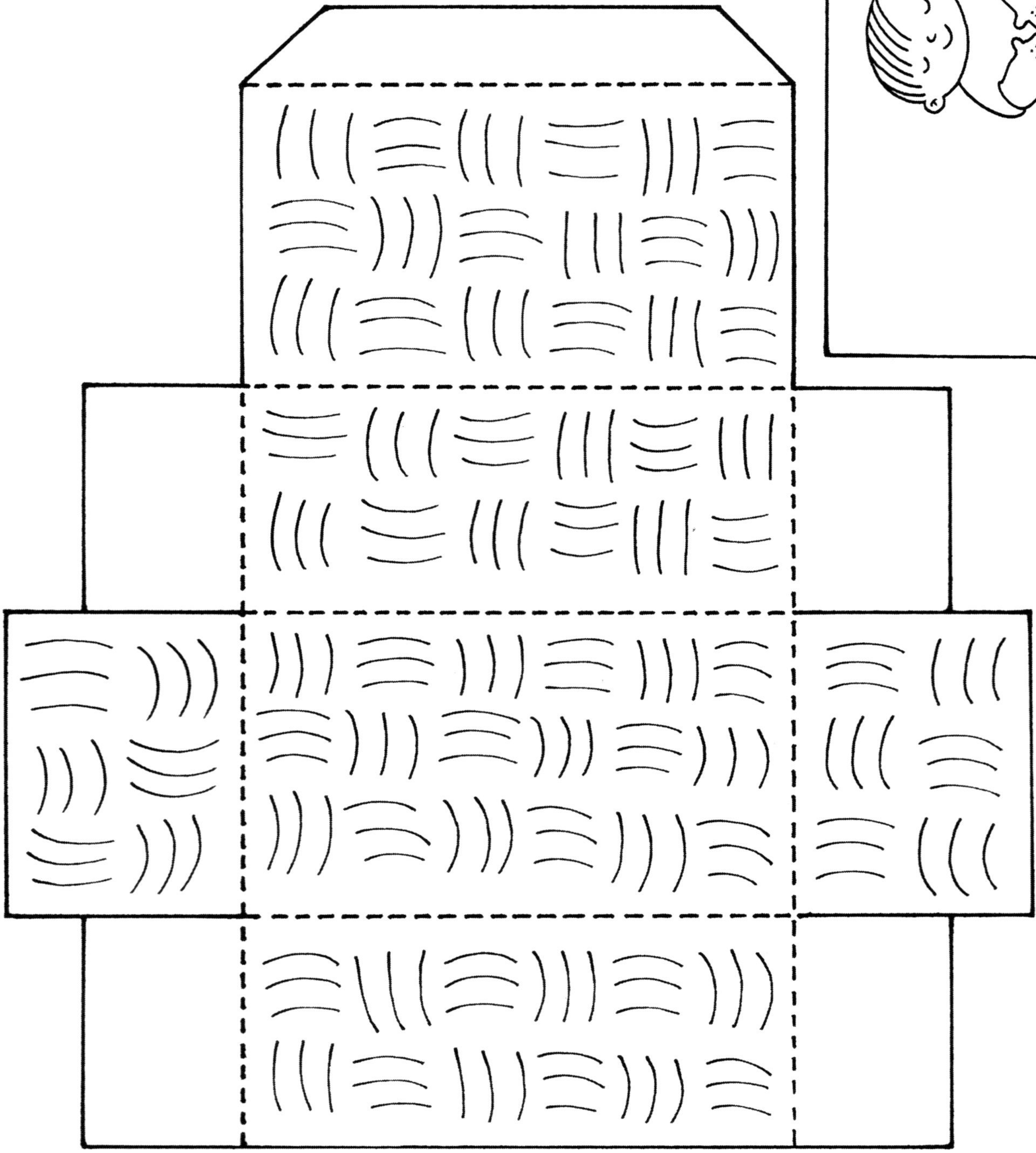

**REPRODUCIBLE 6A**

ALL-IN-ONE BIBLE FUN

One hug at any time

An extra chore with no griping

Ten minutes of quiet time

Help on any job

**69**

# Esther

## Bible Verse

Be strong, and let your heart take courage.

Psalm 27:14

## Bible Story

Esther 1–10

The story of Esther is a story of courage. Esther was chosen to be the new queen of King Ahasuerus, the king of Persia, because of her great beauty. But Esther was more than beautiful; she was courageous.

Haman, the king's prime minister, considered himself to be a very important person, so important that he decided that everyone should worship him. When Mordecai, Esther's cousin, refused, Haman claimed that all the Jews, including Mordecai, were disloyal to the king. He devised a plot to convince the king to order the death of all Jews. When Haman plotted to destroy the Jews, Esther helped her people at the risk of her own life.

Esther went to the king's chambers without being invited, a deed that was punishable by death. But the king felt kindness toward Esther, and Esther invited the king and Haman to a banquet. At that banquet Esther told the king she was a Jew. Then Esther exposed Haman's plot and asked the king to help the Jews.

When the king learned about Haman's plot to kill the Jews, he became enraged. The king ordered Haman killed the same way Haman had planned to kill Mordecai.

Today's Bible story shows a courageous woman who stood up to a government bully who was intent on ridding the world of her people. How often children identify wrongs that are being committed against those less able to stand up for themselves. Children themselves are often shuffled aside even within the church. Encourage your children to be advocates for the downtrodden. As Jesus said, "The Spirit of the Lord is upon me, because he has anointed me to bring good news to the poor" (Luke 4:18).

As a teacher, you can provide a safe arena where children find affirmation and support that will give them courage. Standing up for what is right is easier when one has a sense of being a part of God's family. No matter what the challenge, God will be with us.

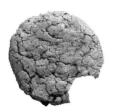

# God helps us stand up for what is right.

If time is limited, we recommend those activities that are noted in **boldface**. Depending on your time and the number of children, you may be able to include more activities.

| ACTIVITY | TIME | SUPPLIES | |
|---|---|---|---|
| **Evil Haman** | **15 minutes** | **Reproducibles 7A and 7B, crayons or felt-tip markers, scissors, masking tape, scarf or bandanna** | JOIN THE FUN |
| If I Ruled the World | 10 minutes | 3 sheets of paper, marker, tape | |
| **Get Into Character** | **10 minutes** | **Bible, mustache (Reproducible 7A), construction paper, newspaper, scissors, tape, crayons or glitter crayons** | BIBLE STORY FUN |
| **Bible Story: Esther, the Queen** | **10 minutes** | **mustache (Reproducible 7A), crown, scepter, pompom** | |
| Sing the Story | 10 minutes | copy of the words | |
| **Heroes for God** | **10 minutes** | **Reproducible 7A, scissors, masking tape** | LIVE THE FUN |

# JOIN THE FUN

## Supplies

Reproducibles 7A and 7B, crayons or felt-tip markers, scissors, masking tape, scarf or bandanna

# Evil Haman

Photocopy one copy of Haman's face **(Reproducible 7B)**. Tape the picture to the wall. Photocopy enough copies of the mustaches **(Reproducible 7A)** so that have mustache for each child.

Let the children cut out the mustaches. Give each child a mustache to color as they wish. Let them put their names on the back.

**Say: In today's Bible story we learn about an evil man named Haman.**

Encourage the children to play "Pin the Mustache on Haman." Have the children bring their mustaches to the game area. Put a rolled piece of masking tape on the back of each mustache. Use a bandanna or scarf to blindfold each child in turn. Let each child try to get Haman's moustache in place.

**Say: In today's Bible story, he does something very wicked because a group of people made him feel less important. But our heroine in the story, Esther, learns that with God's help she can stand up for what is right.**

> **God helps us stand up for what is right.**

## Supplies

3 sheets of paper, marker, tape

# If I Ruled the World

Display three sheets of paper in your storytelling area. At the top of the first sheet of paper write: "Laws I would make." At the top of the second sheet of paper write: "I order people to stop..." At the top of the third sheet of paper write: "I order people to..."

Have the children kneel in front of you. Touch each child on the shoulder.

**Say:** *(Child's name),* **I crown you king/queen of the world for** *(date).*

**Say: You have now been crowned king/queen of the world for one whole day. If this were really true, what laws would you make?** *(Write down what the children suggest.)* **What things would you stop people from doing?** *(Write down the children's suggestions.)* **What things would you order people to do?** *(Write down the children's suggestions.)*

**Say: A good king or queen stands up for what is right. Today we will hear a story about a woman in the Bible who kept a secret. The time came, however, when she had to tell her secret in order to save the lives of her people.**

72

# Get Into Character

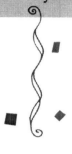

**Supplies**

Bible, mustache (Reproducible 7A), construction paper, newspaper, scissors, tape, crayons or glitter crayons

**Say: You are going to help me tell the story today. It will be like an old-fashioned melodrama, where the whole audience gets involved. First we need to make some props for our melodrama.**

Choose a child to be Esther and make Esther's crown. Give the child a piece of construction paper. Have the child fold the construction paper in half lengthwise. Cut the paper along the fold. Have the child tape the two halves of the paper together to make one long strip. If desired, the child can cut the strips to have points like a tiara. Let the child decorate the crown with crayons or with glitter crayons. Measure the crown around the child's head and tape the ends together.

Choose a child to be the King Ahasuerus and make the king's scepter. Give the child a piece of construction paper. Let the child decorate the paper with crayons or glitter crayons. Show the child how to roll the paper lengthwise into a long tube and tape the edges together.

Choose a child to be Haman. Haman will hold the mustache (**Reproducible 7A**) up to his face.

Choose a child to be Mordecai and make a pompom. Give the child a piece of newspaper. Have the child fold the newspaper in half. Then have the child roll the newspaper into a tube and tape the edges. Show the child how to cut strips ending half way down all around the tube to make the pompom. Mordecai should shake the pompom each time he or she stands.

**Say: As a character, I want you to stand up whenever you hear your name. The rest of you will be the audience and provide the sound effects. Whenever Esther stands up, everyone will stand up and cheer.** (*Practice several times.*) **Whenever I say the king's name, bow or curtsy.** (*Practice several times.*) **Whenever I say Mordecai, chant—Mordecai, Mordecai, he's our man. If he can't do it, no one can!** (*Practice several times.*) **When I say Haman, the wicked, evil Haman, I want you to boo and hiss.** (*Practice several times.*)

Mix up the names several times. Caution the children that in real life, we should never boo or hiss anyone. As you tell the story, pause after each name for the children to perform their part.

**Say: Today's story is in the Old Testament of the Bible. It's about a young woman named Esther. She has a whole book of the Bible named for her.** (*Locate the Book of Esther and show the children where it is. Let one child hold the Bible as you tell the story.*) **It's also about a king named Ahasuerus; a fine, upstanding man named Mordecai; and a wicked, evil government official named Haman.**

# Esther, the Queen

by LeeDell Stickler

**King Ahasuerus** was a very powerful king. One day his wife, Queen Vashti made him very angry. She refused to follow one of his orders. **King Ahasuerus** was not used to having people tell him no. So, he decided to get a new queen.

**King Ahasuerus** invited all the unmarried young women of his kingdom to come to the palace so he could choose a new queen.

**Mordecai**, the palace gatekeeper, had a cousin named **Esther**. **Esther's** parents had died when she was very young and **Mordecai** had raised her as his daughter. Not only was **Esther** beautiful, but she was also kind, loving, and intelligent. "**Esther** would make a wonderful queen," thought **Mordecai**.

So, **Mordecai** urged **Esther** to go before **King Ahasuerus**. But **Mordecai** warned her, "Tell no one of your people. The Jews are not favored in this land. The king may not look upon you kindly if he knows who your people are." And so, **Esther** kept her family a secret.

**Esther** went to the palace with all the other young women. Finally, **King Ahasuerus** made up his mind. "I choose **Esther** to be my queen. She is very beautiful. She is also kind, loving, and intelligent."

**King Ahasuerus** held a great banquet in **Esther's** honor and declared a national holiday. **Esther** was so pleased. But she remembered what **Mordecai** had said to her. She kept her secret safe.

**King Ahasuerus** had a chief officer named **Haman**. **Haman** was cruel. He thought he was very important. **Haman** had **King Ahasuerus** make a law that make all people bow down to **Haman**. So, everyone bowed down—everyone except **Mordecai**. This made **Haman** very angry. But **Mordecai** was a Jew, he bowed to no one but God. So, **Haman** decided to get rid of **Mordecai** and his people.

**Haman** came before **King Ahasuerus**, "O Great King, did you know there are people in your land who have their own laws and do not keep your law? You should get rid of them."

King Ahasuerus trusted Haman. He did not want these troublesome people in his land. "Do to these people what you want to," said the king.

When Mordecai heard what Haman planned to do, he cried out, "Our people are in trouble. Queen Esther is our only hope. She must get King Ahasuerus to change his mind."

When Esther heard what Mordecai wanted her to do, she was afraid. "If I go to the king without being called, he will be very angry. He could kill me!"

"I believe God has a plan for you," Mordecai said to his cousin. "Perhaps this is the reason you became queen."

Esther knew what she must do. She bravely went before King Ahasuerus. Instead of being angry, the king was happy to see her. He held out his royal scepter to her. "What do you wish, my queen?"

"Please come to a banquet. And bring Haman with you," said Esther.

King Ahasuerus agreed. Haman felt even more important than usual.

That night at the banquet, King Ahasuerus said, "Esther, tell me your wish. I will grant it."

"My king, if you are pleased with me, save my life and the lives of my people!" Esther fell to her knees.

"What are you talking about?" King Ahasuerus asked. "Who would dare harm my queen and her people?"

"An order went out that my people and I are to be killed. Please save us!" Esther begged.

"Who ordered such a thing?" the king demanded.

Esther pointed at Haman. "This wicked man!" Haman knew that he was in deep trouble.

King Ahasuerus jumped up from the table. He paced back and forth trying to decide what to do. Then he ordered: "What Haman had planned for you and for all your people shall now be done to him!"

Then the king ordered messengers to go throughout the kingdom to undo what he had unknowingly ordered.

So, because of Queen Esther, the Jewish people were saved. King Ahasuerus rewarded Esther for her courage and made Mordecai his new chief officer.

# BIBLE STORY FUN

## Supplies

copy of words

# Sing the Story

Photocopy the words to the song "Esther True and Grand-y" printed below. Give each child a copy.

### God helps us stand up for what is right.

Sing the song to the tune of "Yankee Doodle."

**Esther True and Grand-y**

Haman was an evil man,
so hateful and despise-y
he plotted for all Jews to die;
The king was none the wise-y.

**Chorus:**
**Esther was a shining star!**
**Esther was a dandy!**
**Though she wore a royal crown,**
**She stayed so true and grand-y.**

Esther learned from Mordecai
of Haman's wicked deal-y
She bravely went before the king;
On Haman she did squeal-y.

**Chorus**

Now the Jews in all the lands
do honor Esther dearly
With Purim feasts and gifts and games
they celebrate her yearly.

**Chorus**

Words: Nancy Ashley Young
Words © 1989 Graded Press

ALL-IN-ONE BIBLE FUN

# Heroes for God

Photocopy and cut out the badge **(Reproducible 7A)** for each child.

Say: Whenever we stand up for what is right, we are being heroes for God. We are showing other people how Christians live. This is not always easy.

Ask: Have you ever had friends make fun of you because you wouldn't do something that you knew was wrong? Or have friends every made fun of you because you did something that they thought was "uncool"?

Say: I'm going to read about a person. If the person in the story stood up for God, then stand up and say the Bible verse: "Be strong, and let your heart take courage" (Psalm 27:14). If the person did not act in a way Christians should respond, stomp your feet.

1. Josie's friends thought it would be fun to write their names on the school sidewalk. When the gang handed Josie the paint, she wrote her name, too.
2. Elizabeth put part of her allowance in the church offering.
3. Jason made fun of a boy in his class who couldn't catch the ball.
4. Libby made brownies with her mother and carried them to a neighbor who was ill.
5. Alex invited the "new kid" to eat lunch with him and his friends.

Invite the children to share experiences where they have had to stand up for what is right.

Say: You can be a hero for God. You can stand up for what's right, even when other people are doing what's wrong. You can do what's right when other people aren't doing anything at all. God will be with you and help you do what's right. One way all of you stood up for God today is by coming here today.

Place a loop of tape on the back of each badge. Give each child a badge to wear.

Say: (Child's name), I award you this ribbon for bravery. Today you stood up for God.

Pray: God, sometimes it isn't easy to do what's right. Sometimes we may be afraid or embarrassed. We want to do what's right. Each of us will whisper something that is particularly hard for us to do. (*Invite the children to whisper something they find hard to do.*) Help us this week. Amen.

**REPRODUCIBLE 7A**

ALL-IN-ONE BIBLE FUN

Heroes of the Bible - Elementary

All-in-One
BIBLE ELEMENTARY
FUN

# Jesus and the Children

## Bible Verse

Let the little children come to me; do not stop them; for it is to such as these that the kingdom of God belongs.

Mark 10:14

## Bible Story

Mark 10:13-16

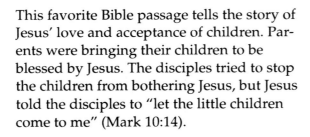

This favorite Bible passage tells the story of Jesus' love and acceptance of children. Parents were bringing their children to be blessed by Jesus. The disciples tried to stop the children from bothering Jesus, but Jesus told the disciples to "let the little children come to me" (Mark 10:14).

Jesus was indignant when he stopped his friends from sending the children away. His attitude must have been hard for his friends to understand. Children, like women, had few personal rights in Bible times. Jesus' friends probably thought the children were not important enough to interrupt Jesus. After all, crowds of adults had come to hear Jesus teach. But Jesus had a way of turning around common practices. He must have surprised

everyone when he stopped what he was doing to spend time with children.

Jesus told the crowd gathered to hear him teach that the kingdom of God belongs to children. He wanted the people to realize that the characteristics of children—their sense of wonder, their innocence, their ability to forgive quickly—were characteristics that everyone needed in order to be part of God's kingdom.

Jesus welcomed the children and showed them what God's love was like by touching them and blessing them. As teachers you have the opportunity to show the children you teach what God's love is like. When you are patient, kind, consistent, and respectful with your children, you are modeling God's love.

# We know Jesus loves us and that we are important to God.

If time is limited, we recommend those activities that are noted in **boldface**. Depending on your time and the number of children, you may be able to include more activities.

| ACTIVITY | TIME | SUPPLIES | |
|---|---|---|---|
| **Welcome All God's Children** | **10 minutes** | **Reproducible 8A, construction paper, scissors, crayons or felt-tip markers, glue, tape** | JOIN THE FUN |
| Jesus Loves… | 10 minutes | Reproducible 8B, white crayons, watercolor paints, brushes, cups of water, paint smocks, table covering | |
| Obstacles | 10 minutes | items to create an obstacle course, such as tables, chairs, sheets or fabric, boxes, crepe paper streamers | BIBLE STORY FUN |
| Sing Jesus Loves Me | 5 minutes | None | |
| **Bible Story: Jesus Says Yes** | **10 minutes** | **copies of the story, poster-board, marker, Bible-times costumes** | |
| Chant the Story | 5 minutes | None | |
| Loving Hands, Loving Hearts | 10 minutes | construction paper, scissors, crayons or felt-tip markers, large piece of paper, masking tape, glue | LIVE THE FUN |
| **Important Prayers** | **5 minutes** | **None** | |

Heroes of the Bible - Elementary

# JOIN THE FUN

## Welcome All God's Children

### Supplies

Reproducible 8A, construction paper, scissors, crayons or felt-tip markers, glue, tape

Photocopy the welcome sign **(Reproducible 8A)** for each child.

Greet each child as he or she arrives. Give each child the welcome sign. Let the children decorate the signs with crayons or felt-tip markers. Encourage each child to sign his or her name on the sign.

Let each child choose a favorite color of construction paper. Have the children glue the signs onto the colored paper.

**Say: Today our Bible story is a well-known story about how Jesus welcomed the children. Jesus' friends thought that children were not important enough to see Jesus. But Jesus showed his friends that children were important to God and important to him. Let's place our signs around our church to welcome everyone — men, women, and children.**

Take the children to post the signs around your church.

> # We know Jesus loves us and that we are important to God.

## Jesus Loves...

### Supplies

Reproducible 8B, white crayons, watercolor paints, brushes, cups of water, paint smocks, table covering

Photocopy Jesus loves… **(Reproducible 8B)** for each child. Use a white crayon to write the child's name in the heart, pressing hard.

Cover the table. Have the children wear paint smocks to protect their clothing. Set out watercolor paints and cups of water.

Give each child the paper with his or her name printed in white crayon. Let the children paint over the page with water colors. The paint will not cover the crayon writing, thus revealing each child's name.

**Say: Our Bible story tells us that Jesus thought children were just as important as adults. We know that Jesus loves each one of us. Each and every one of us is important to God.**

82

# Obstacles

Help the children create an obstacle course that they must cross in order to get to the Bible story area. They can crawl under tables, over chairs, around bookcases, under sheets or fabric, or through boxes or crepe paper streamers.

Be sure that the obstacle course is safe and can be completed by every child.

Once they have created the obstacle course, have the children move to the beginning of the course.

**Say: We must all get through the obstacle course successfully before we can hear today's Bible story.**

Encourage the children to help one another get through the course safely.

**Ask: What was the hardest part of the course? What was the easiest? Was going through the course fun? Why did you want to get to the end of the course?**

**Say: In today's Bible story the children wanted to go to Jesus, but they found an obstacle in their way.**

# Sing Jesus Loves Me

Divide the children into two groups. Have the groups stand at opposite ends of the room and face each other.

Have the groups alternate singing the phrases of the song.

**For example:**

**Group 1** - Jesus loves me! This I know,

**Group 2** - For the Bible tells me so.

Teach the children a simple body rhythm. Sing the song again and have the children repeat the rhythm throughout the song.

| Text | Action |
| --- | --- |
| Jesus | stomp twice |
| Loves me! | pat thighs twice |
| This I | clap twice |
| Know | snap once |

**83**

# Jesus Says Yes

by Sandy Mabry and Sally Johnson

Make two signs for the prompter. Sign 1: Yeah! Sign 2: Boo!

Photocopy "Jesus Says Yes" for the children. Choose children to play these roles: Jesus, parents, 2 or 3 children, 3 disciples, and prompter. Children without specific parts will be the crowd.

Have Jesus, the parents, children, and disciples wear costumes if desired.

Give the prompter the signs made earlier.

*(Parents and children are gathered on one side of the stage area. The disciples are on the opposite side.)*

**Disciple One:** I'm so tired.

**Disciple Two:** Me too. Traveling from town to town is hard work.

**Disciple Three:** Even though it is great to be with Jesus, I'm so tired. I need a long nap.

*(Jesus Enters)*

*(Prompter holds up sign: Yeah!)*

**Jesus:** Hello, my friends. What a great day we've had! *(Disciples nod their heads.)* It makes me happy to see people hearing God's Word.

*(The children rush over and surround Jesus.)*

**Child One:** Hello, Jesus!

**Child Two:** I love you, Jesus!

*(Prompter holds up sign: Yeah!)*

*(The disciples rush to the children and send them back to their parents.)*

**Disciple One:** Stop crowding around Jesus!

**Disciple Two:** Can't you see he is too tired to mess with you?

ALL-IN-ONE BIBLE FUN

**Disciple Three:** Jesus doesn't have time for little children! He's got more important things to do.

*(Prompter holds up sign: Boo!)*
*(The children turn and walk slowly back to their parents.)*

**Jesus:** Stop!

**Disciples:** What? What did we do? Did we do something wrong?

**Jesus:** Do not stop the children from coming near me! Children are special people to God. These children are God's children, just like you.

*(Prompter holds up sign: Yeah!)*

**Disciple One:** But Jesus, they are just little children.

*(Prompter holds up sign: Boo!)*

**Disciple Two:** There are many more important people wanting to talk to you.

*(Prompter holds up sign: Boo!)*

**Disciple Three:** Let's send them back to their parents where they belong.

*(Prompter holds up sign: Boo!)*

*(A parent steps forward.)*

**Parent One:** We walked a long way to have Jesus bless our children.

**Parent Two:** We have waited all day.

**Jesus:** *(turns to the disciples)* My friends, God wants us to welcome these children in the same way we would welcome kings and queens. These children have special gifts to offer the family of God. We must not turn them away.

*(Prompter holds up sign: Yeah!)*

**Parent One:** Jesus, will you bless our children?

**Jesus:** Come to me.

*(Parents and children go to Jesus.)*

**Jesus:** I bless you, children. I bless your parents and everyone who cares for you. May my disciples always remember that you are important to God.

*(Prompter holds up sign: Yeah!)*

adapted from *PowerXpress! Jesus and the Children*. 2005 Abingdon Press.

## Supplies

None

# Chant the Story

Teach the words and rhythm of the story. Then teach the motions to go with the words. This is a call and response chant. You will speak the part in bold print and do the motions. The children will repeat the words and motions after you.

**Say: Let's tell the story again. This time I want you to listen to me and then repeat what I say.**

**The children said; yes, the children said:** *(Shake head, "yes.")*
**Hey, Jesus!** *(Raise hand in the air.)* **Hey, Jesus!** *(Raise hand in the air.)*

*(Children repeat)*

**The disciples said; no, the disciples said:** *(Shake head, "no.")*
**Stop children!** *(Hold up palm to say stop.)* **Stop children!** *(Hold up palm.)*

*(Children repeat)*

**The children said; yes, the children said:** *(Shake head, "yes.")*
**Look, Jesus!** *(Wave.)* **Look, Jesus!** *(Wave.)*

*(Children repeat)*

**Jesus said; yes, Jesus said:** *(Shake head, "yes.")*
**Come, children!** *(Motion, "come here.")* **Come, children!** *(Motion, "come here.")*

*(Children repeat)*

**The children said; yes, the children said:** *(Shake head, "yes.")*
**We love you!** *(Cross hands over heart.)* **We love you!** *(Cross hands over heart.)*

*(Children repeat)*

**The disciples said; yes, the disciples said:** *(Shake head, "yes.")*
**Come children!** *(Motion, "come here.")* **Come children!** *(Motion, "come here.")*

*(Children repeat)*

**Jesus said; yes, Jesus said:** *(Shake head, "yes.")*
**Bless the children!** *(Cross hands over heart.)* **Bless the children!** *(Cross hands over heart.)*

> **We know Jesus loves us and that we are important to God.**

# Loving Hands, Loving Hearts

**Supplies**

construction paper, scissors, crayons or felt-tip markers, large piece of paper, masking tape, glue

Help each child trace his or her hands on a piece of construction paper. Children may help each other do the tracings.

Have the children cut out their hand tracings. Let them decorate their handprints with crayons or markers.

Draw the outline of a heart on a large piece of paper. Or use masking tape to make the outline of a large heart on the wall or door.

Have the children glue or tape their handprints on to the heart outline.

Say: Our Bible story today is about a time when Jesus showed God's love to children. Children were not very important in Bible times. Jesus showed the children that they were important to God and to him.

Ask: Have you ever felt unimportant? When?

Say: You are important!

We know Jesus loves us and that we are important to God.

# Important Prayers

**Supplies**

None

Have the children sit in a circle. Encourage the children to look closely at their thumbs and then at the palms of their hands. Tell the children to compare their hands with the hands of their neighbors.

Choose a child to stand up.

Say: *(Child's name)* you are important to God and to us.

Continue with each child and teacher in the circle.

Say: None of you has thumbs or hands that are just alike, but each one of you is a child of God. You are all special and you all have an important place in God's family.

Pray: Thank you, God, for *(name each child and teacher in the circle)*. Help each of us remember that we are important to you. Amen.

**87**

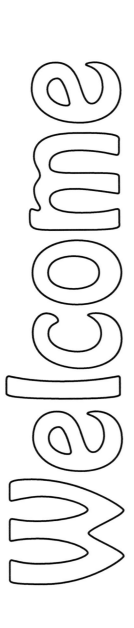

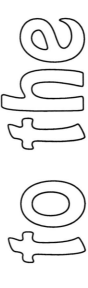

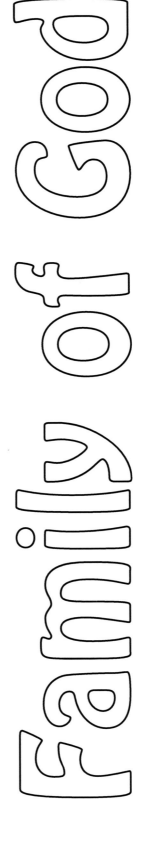

Welcome to the Family of God

**REPRODUCIBLE 8A**

ALL-IN-ONE BIBLE FUN

# Jesus loves

# A Boy and His Lunch

## Bible Verse

Do not neglect to do good and to share what you have, for such sacrifices are pleasing to God.

Hebrews 13:16

## Bible Story

John 6:1-14

Once there were more than five thousand people who wanted to be with Jesus. Some were sick and wanted Jesus to heal them. Others wanted to hear Jesus talk about God and God's love.

When evening came, Jesus knew these people were hungry. Jesus asked his disciples to feed everyone, but they didn't know how to do it. "We didn't bring any food," they said, "and we don't have enough money to buy supper for this many people."

Then a little boy in the crowd said, "I have five loaves of bread and two fish. I'll share." But the disciples said, "That's not enough to go around."

Like the disciples, we often view life through the lens of limitations. We look at the great needs in the world and feel inadequate to meet those needs. We focus on what we're lacking. We look at the impossible nature of a situation and say, "I can't do anything to make a difference. I don't have enough to offer."

But God invites us to look at life through a lens of abundance, generosity, and possibility. When we're faced with a difficult situation, we can offer to give and do what we can, regardless of how little it seems.

Our God is a God of miraculous power! God can use our gift, no matter how large or small, to help meet the needs of others.

# Jesus taught us to share with others.

If time is limited, we recommend those activities that are noted in **boldface**. Depending on your time and the number of children, you may be able to include more activities.

| ACTIVITY | TIME | SUPPLIES | |
|---|---|---|---|
| **A Lunch for Sharing** | **10 minutes** | **Reproducible 9A, scissors, paper punch, masking tape, crayons or felt-tip markers, yarn** | JOIN THE FUN |
| Multiply God's Love | 10 minutes | Scrip, Loaves and Fishes Cards (Reproducible 9A), large brown grocery bag, folded newspapers, masking tape | BIBLE STORY FUN |
| **Bible Story: Jesus, the Teacher** | **10 minutes** | **None** | |
| Hidden in the Crowd | 5 minutes | Reproducible 9B, crayons or markers | |
| Sing the Story | 5 minutes | None | |
| Volleyball Verses | 10 minutes | Bible, chairs, beach ball or balloon | LIVE THE FUN |
| **Share a Prayer** | **5 minutes** | **slips of paper, basket, pencils** | |

# JOIN THE FUN

## Supplies

Reproducible 9A, scissors, paper punch, masking tape, crayons or felt-tip markers, yarn

# A Lunch for Sharing

Photocopy the lunch pouch and the loaves and fishes cards (**Reproducible 9A**) for each child. A *scrip* is a leather pouch. The boy in the Bible story might have carried his lunch in a scrip.

Greet the children as they arrive.

**Say: Today we are going to hear a story about a special lunch and how it multiplied to feed more than five thousand people. We might wonder how that happened. But with God anything is possible. God took a small boy's gift and multiplied it many times. God can do that with what we have to share, too.**

## Jesus taught us to share with others.

Have each child cut out the scrip and the loaves and fishes cards. Let the children decorate the scrip and the cards with crayons or felt-tip markers. Set the loaves and fishes cards aside.

Show each child how to fold the scrip and punch holes along the edge. Cut the yarn into one-yard lengths, one for each child. Wrap the end with a piece of masking tape to make it easy to use. Then, leaving a twelve-inch tail, lace the scrip together. Tie the end pieces together, forming a handle that will fit easily over a child's head, and let the scrip hang down.

Have the children place the loaves and fishes cards in their pouches.

92

# Multiply God's Love

**Supplies**

Scrip, Loaves and Fishes Cards (Reproducible 9A), large brown grocery bag, folded newspapers, masking tape

Bring the children together in a circle. Place the open grocery sack in the center of the circle. Put the folded up newspaper inside.

**Ask: Does the sack look full or empty?** (*It looks fairly empty.*) **Is there room for anything else?** (*Yes.*)

**Say: Actually, we can fix it so the bag is full to overflowing without adding a single thing.**

Unfold the newspaper and give each child several sheets. Have the children crumple the newspaper into balls and then place them in the sack. By the time all the sheets are added to the sack, it should be totally full.

**Ask: What happened?** (*The bag is now overflowing.*) **Is there more newspaper in the bag?** (*No, we just made it bigger.*)

**Say: In today's Bible story, Jesus takes a small amount of food and multiplies it many, many times until there is enough to feed the whole crowd and have much left over. That's what happens when with God's power you share.**

**Say: Let's play a game. The object is for you to get rid of all of your loaves and fishes (Reproducible 9A). You must give them away.**

Have the children stand up and remove the loaves and fishes from their lunch pouch. Put loops of masking tape on the back of each.

**Say: When I say one at a time you will give away your lunch by taping it to someone else's lunch pouch. But other people will be giving away theirs at the same time. Let's see what happens.**

Say, "Go," and let the children proceed to try to give away their loaves and fishes. After a few minutes call, "Stop."

**Ask: What happened?** (*We gave them away, but more kept coming back.*)

**Say: That's what happens when you share. The more you give away, the more keeps coming back to you. Jesus taught the people this important lesson about sharing.**

**Jesus taught us to share with others.**

93

# Jesus, the Teacher

by LeeDell Stickler

> **Say:** You are going to help me tell the story. I will give you certain words to listen for. You must listen very carefully. When you hear these words, you will do certain actions.
>
> Introduce the words and have the children practice the actions.
>
> **Follow:** Everyone stands up and walks in place.
> **Boat:** Everyone pretends to row a boat.
> **Tired:** Everyone yawns.
> **Hungry:** Everyone pats stomach and says, "Yum, yum."
> **Five thousand:** Everyone grabs head and says, "Five thousand!"
> **Money:** Everyone holds out hand and pretends to count coins.
> **Share:** Everyone pretends to hand out objects.
> **Miracle:** Everyone falls down to his or her knees and folds hands.

Everywhere Jesus went, many would **follow**. They would **follow** him down the road. They would **follow** him in the cities. They would **follow** him in the countryside. Jesus could never get away from the people.

One day when Jesus was particularly **tired**, he and his friends got into a **boat** to get away. But the people on the shore soon spotted the **boat** and began to **follow** along the lakeshore. When Jesus and his friends put the **boat** onto the beach, the people were there waiting for him.

Jesus felt sorry for them and did not send them away. Some had come a long distance just to hear him. So, he gathered them together and began to teach them. All day people long more and more people came to see him. Soon there were at least **five thousand** people.

Some people wanted Jesus to heal them. Some people wanted Jesus to bless them. Other people came to hear Jesus teach them about God.

When Jesus finished teaching the people, it was late in the day. Jesus

ALL-IN-ONE BIBLE FUN

was **tired**. Jesus' friends were **tired**. The people were **tired**. And everyone was **hungry**.

"What are we going to do about food?" asked one of Jesus' friends. "It is getting late, time for the evening meal, and there is nothing here for the people to eat. I am certain that the people are **hungry**. Shall I send them into the nearby village for bread?"

"No, " said Jesus. "We should provide for them. They are **tired** and **hungry**. They have come a long way just to hear me."

"We do not have enough **money** to buy bread, even a small amount, for such a large number of people. There must be **five thousand** people here. What shall we do?"

Just then the disciples heard a small voice. The men looked down and saw a small boy. He held out his leather lunch pouch. "Here," he said, "I will **share** my lunch."

The boy had come to see Jesus. He had **followed** along with the crowd. He had brought with him a small lunch of five barley loaves and two dried fish, just enough food for one small boy, hardly enough for the **five thousand** men,

women, and children who had gathered there. But still he held out his lunch to Jesus. He was willing to **share** what he had.

Jesus looked at the boy and thought for a moment. "Have the people sit down on the grass," said Jesus. Then Jesus took the boy's lunch. He gave thanks to God and broke the bread. When the food was **shared**, there was enough for everyone.

When the people had eaten all they cared to eat, Jesus told his friends, "Gather up what is left over. We do not want to waste any."

The disciples passed through the crowd, collecting the leftover bread and fish. There were twelve full baskets left over. It was a **miracle**!

When the people saw the **miracle**, they knew that they had seen something wonderful. They exclaimed out loud, "This is indeed the one who the Scriptures said was coming."

## Supplies

Reproducible
9B, crayons or
markers

# Hidden in the Crowd

Photocopy the hidden picture (Reproducible 9B) for each child. Have the children find the loaves and fish hidden in the picture. Let the children decorate the picture with crayons or markers.

Ask: Which person in the picture do you think represents Jesus? How do you think Jesus felt when he saw all the people following him? Which person do you think is the boy who shared his lunch? How do you think he felt when Jesus took his two fish and five loaves of bread? How do you think the people felt after they had eaten as much food as they wanted?

## Supplies

None

# Sing the Story

Sing the song printed below to tune of "She'll Be Coming Round the Mountain."

## The Boy's Lunch

Oh, Jesus taught the people all day
    long.
Oh, Jesus taught the people all day
    long.
From the morning to the evening,
From the morning to the evening.
Oh, Jesus taught the people all day
    long.

Oh, the people they were getting
    hungry now.
Oh, the people they were getting
    hungry now.
It was time to eat some supper,
It was time to eat some supper.
Oh, the people they were getting
    hungry now.

Oh, Jesus said to give the people food.
Oh, Jesus said to give the people food.
Then he turned to his disciples,
Then he turned to his disciples.
Oh, Jesus said to give the people food.

Then a boy said, "I will share my
    lunch with you."
Then a boy said, "I will share my
    lunch with you."
"I have barley loaves and fishes,
I have barley loaves and fishes."

Then a boy said, "I will share my
    lunch with you."

Oh, Jesus told the people to sit down.
Oh, Jesus told the people to sit down.
Then he thanked God for the fishes,
Then he thanked God for the fishes.
Oh, Jesus told the people to sit down.

Now everyone was fed from that
    small lunch.
Now everyone was fed from that
    small lunch.
Just five barley loaves and fishes,
Just five barley loaves and fishes,
Now everyone was fed from that
    small lunch.

Twelve baskets were left over from
    that lunch.
Twelve baskets were left over from
    that lunch.
After everyone had eaten,
After everyone had eaten,
Twelve baskets were left over from
    that lunch.

Words: Daphna Flegal
Words © 2001 Abingdon Press

# Volleyball Verses

Read Hebrews 13:16. Repeat the verse together: "Do not neglect to do good and to share what you have, for such sacrifices are pleasing to God" (Hebrews 13:16).

Count off by two's to divide into two groups.

Split an open area of the room into two sides for a "volleyball" court. Put chairs in the middle for the "net."

Have one team serve the beach ball or balloon. The receiving team tries to hit the ball back across the net and say the first word of the verse. Continue hitting the ball back and forth, adding another word each time until the verse has been repeated correctly.

**Supplies**

Bible, chairs, beach ball or balloon

# Share a Prayer

**Say: Jesus cares about our needs, just as he cared about the needs of those five thousand people.**

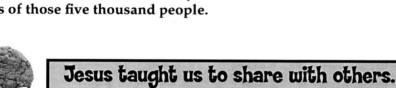

Jesus taught us to share with others.

**Say: One way we can help and share with others is by praying.**

Hand out slips of paper. Have each child write his or her name on a slip and fold the slip in half.

Place all the slips in a basket and mix them up.

Pass the basket around, having each person take a slip, checking to make sure they do not have their own name.

Instruct the children to find the person whose name they picked, and ask them if they have a special prayer request.

Encourage the children to pray for the person whose name they picked every day for a week.

**Pray: Loving God, thank you for Jesus and the many ways he taught us about your love. I ask your blessing upon *(say the names of each person in the group)*. Help them show your love to others by sharing. Amen.**

**Supplies**

slips of paper, basket, pencils

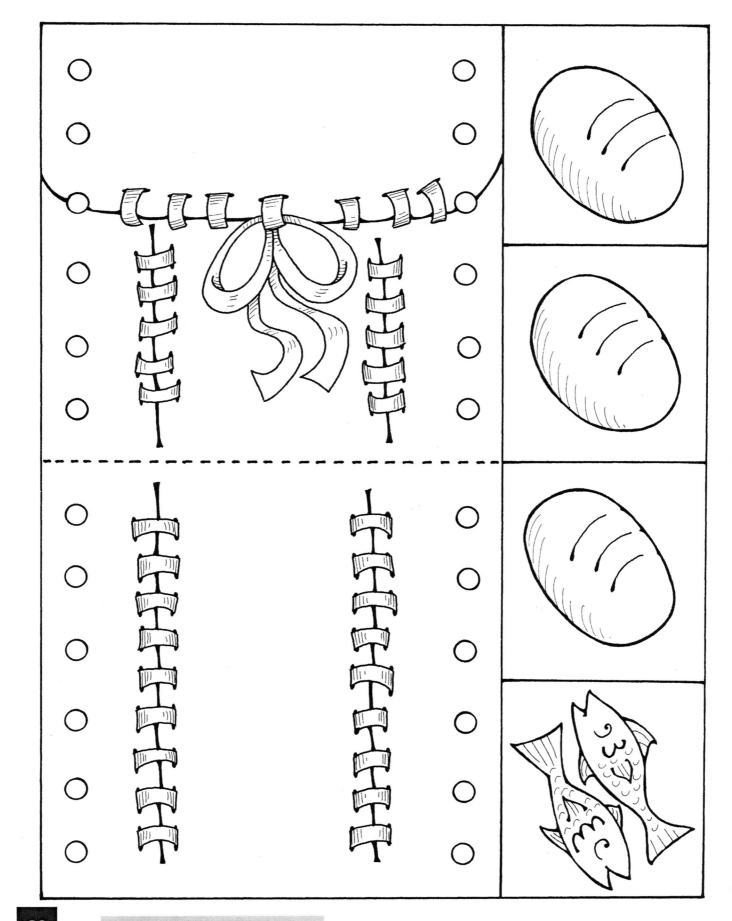

**REPRODUCIBLE 9A**

Permission granted to photocopy for local church use. © 1997, 2010 Abingdon Press.

ALL-IN-ONE BIBLE FUN

# Peter and John

## Bible Verse

Just as you did it to one of the least of these who are members of my family, you did it to me.

Matthew 25:40

## Bible Story

### Acts 3:1-16

Today's story is about Peter and John and the healing of a man who could not walk. Peter and John were going to the Temple to pray. They passed by a man sitting at the gate of the Temple. Because the man could not walk his friends would carry him to the gate so that he could beg for money. When he saw Peter and John, he asked them for money. Peter replied, "I have no silver or gold, but what I have I give you; in the name of Jesus Christ of Nazareth, stand up and walk" (Acts 3:6). The man immediately stood up and entered the Temple, leaping and praising God.

This healing miracle took place after Pentecost. It was at Pentecost that Jesus' followers received the gift of the Holy Spirit. The Holy Spirit filled with power the frightened band of followers who hid after the Crucifixion and Resurrection. They now preached and taught and healed without fear.

Peter and John were two of Jesus' closest followers. The man that Peter and John saw at the gate to the city had been unable to walk since birth. He was not able to work and had to beg for money to buy food. Instead of money, however, Peter healed the man in the name of Jesus. Peter and John wanted everyone to understand that the man was healed by the power of Jesus.

Children at this age enjoy helping. In fact, their enthusiasm for helping often exceeds their ability to perform the desired task. But do not discourage them. If a child is made to feel that his help is unwanted or inadequate, he or she will soon quit offering. Encourage helping activities in a class. Accept your children's gifts of help.

Remind your children that with God all things are possible. One important way they can help others is through prayer. They may not be able to heal the sick, but they can pray for persons who are ill.

# We can help one another.

If time is limited, we recommend those activities that are noted in **boldface**. Depending on your time and the number of children, you may be able to include more activities.

| ACTIVITY | TIME | SUPPLIES | |
|---|---|---|---|
| **Clean-up Time** | **10 minutes** | **newspaper, spray cleaner, sponges, paper towels** | JOIN THE FUN |
| Stand Together | 5 minutes | None | |
| Helper Ball | 10 minutes | large piece of paper or towel for each child, beach ball or foam ball | BIBLE STORY FUN |
| **Bible Story: Peter and John** | **10 minutes** | **None** | |
| Get Up and Walk | 10 minutes | beanbag or scarf | |
| Sing the Story | 5 minutes | None | |
| Help Me, Please! | 10 minutes | Reproducibles 10A and 10B, scissors | LIVE THE FUN |
| **Helping Hand Prayers** | **5 minutes** | **construction paper, scissors, felt-tip marker, ruler** | |

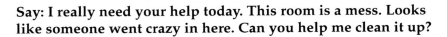

## Supplies

newspaper,
spray cleaner,
sponges,
paper towels

# Clean-up Time

Prior to the children's arrival, wad up newspaper and scatter it around the room. Make sure there is plenty.

Say: I really need your help today. This room is a mess. Looks like someone went crazy in here. Can you help me clean it up?

Involve the children in picking up newspaper, using spray cleaner to clean the tables and wipe off the chairs. As each new child enters the room, find a task that he or she can do. Work to get the room in order.

When everything is clean and straight, have the children come together.

Say: Thanks for helping me. I couldn't have done the job alone. And when you helped me, it made the job more fun and easier.

Ask: How did you feel about helping? Do you help at home? What kinds of jobs do you do?

Say: In today's Bible story, we hear about two of Jesus' friends who helped someone in a special way. The Bible message speaks to us, too. The Bible teaches us that:

> ## We can help one another.

## Supplies

None

# Stand Together

Have the children sit on the floor and put their knees to their chests.

Challenge the children to stand up without using their hands. (They will not be able to stand.)

Say: I need this group to stand. No hands may touch the floor. Work together to figure out a way for everyone to stand.

Let the children puzzle out a way to stand up. Some children will realize that if two people sit back to back and lock arms, they will be able to push against their partner's back and stand.

Ask: Did you need help? Everyone needs help sometime. Who helped you? When do you help someone else?

# Helper Ball

**Supplies**

large piece of paper or towel for each child, beach ball or foam ball

Give each child a large piece of paper or a towel to use as a stretcher. Have the children spread their stretchers out on the floor in a circle. Then have the children sit down on their stretchers.

Say: Let's take a look at our hands and feet. Hold up your hands. Your hand has twenty-seven bones. Just your four fingers and your thumb have fourteen bones. Make a claw shape with one of your hands. Count each bend in your fingers and thumbs. Between each bend is a knuckle. Count your knuckles.

Say: Now take off your shoes and socks so you can look at your feet. (Don't force any child who doesn't want to remove his shoes or socks.) Your foot has twenty-six bones. Wiggle your toes. Move your foot in a circle. The many bones in your hands and feet are held together by ligaments, tendons, and muscles.

Say: Place your hands on the floor beside your feet. Move your thumbs to point to the side. Your thumb does something your big toe can't do. It can move in a different direction from your fingers. This lets you pick things up and hold things with your hands.

Say: Today our Bible story is about a man who could not walk. He could not wiggle his toes or move his foot in a circle. Because he could not walk, he could not work. Everyday his friends would carrying him on a stretcher and place him on the ground by the Temple gate. He would beg for money from the people who were going to the Temple.

Say: Let's pretend we cannot move our legs. Sit down on your stretchers. We're going to toss the ball to each other, but you cannot move off your stretcher to get the ball. If the ball rolls out of the circle, our runner will have to get it. Remember, you cannot move off your stretcher.

Choose one child to be the runner. Have the runner stand outside the circle.

Let the children toss the beach ball to one another. When someone misses the ball, the runner goes after the ball and tosses it back to the circle.

Ask: Who helped keep the game going? How did that person help? What are some ways we can help others?

## We can help one another.

# Peter and John

by LeeDell Stickler

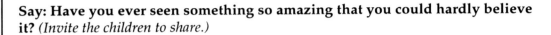

> **Say: Have you ever seen something so amazing that you could hardly believe it?** *(Invite the children to share.)*
>
> Have the children sit down on the floor in a circle. At a certain point in the story, the children will link arms around the circle and sway first to the right, then to the left. Do the motion as the children say the following verse:
>
> **Peter and John, Peter and John,**
> **Special friends of Jesus.**
> **Told the good news of Jesus the Christ**
> **To all who would stop and listen.**
>
> Let the children practice several times. Then tell the story.

Peter and John were two of Jesus' disciples. They were also Jesus' good friends. They had been with Jesus for a long time. They had heard what Jesus taught. They had seen Jesus heal. They had been there when Jesus had been crucified and had risen from the dead. They were part of Jesus' special friends. *(Sway and say.)*

When Jesus left this earth to go and be with God, Jesus told them, "Go and tell all the earth every thing that I have told you. And remember, I am with you, always, even to the end of the world." And that is just what Jesus' friends set out to do. *(Sway and say.)*

One day Peter and John were going to the Temple at the hour of prayer. (Did you know that in Bible times people prayed at certain times of the day? These times were set aside by law. Everyone did it, just as the law prescribed.) As they went into the city, they passed by a man who was sitting on a pallet at the entrance to the Beautiful Gate. *(Sway and say.)*

The man was sitting, because he could not walk. He was sitting in that particular spot because he could not walk and could not work. Every day people had to walk past him and he could ask them for money. It was in the law

ALL-IN-ONE BIBLE FUN

of the people that they were to care for the poor. How lonely the man must have felt!

As Peter and John passed by, the man called out to them, "Alms for the poor. Help a man who cannot walk." The man stretched out his hand toward the two friends of Jesus. *(Sway and say.)*

Peter walked over to the man. The man held out his hands to receive the coins he hoped Peter would drop into them. But instead of giving the man coins, Peter reached out and took him by the hand. "I have no silver or gold, but what I have I give to you. In the name of Jesus Christ, get up and walk." *(Sway and say.)*

Immediately, the man's feet and ankles who grew strong. Jumping up, he stood and began to walk. He began to run. He began to leap and jump for joy, praising God. The people who had been standing around the saw what happened. They were filled with great wonder. "Isn't this the man who cannot walk, the one who begs for alms each day?" *(Sway and say.)*

"Look, look!" some shouted. "The lame man is leaping and dancing and jumping."

The people gathered around Peter and John. They wanted to see the men who had done such a wondrous thing.

"Why are you surprised?" Peter asked them. "We do not do this by our own power. The power of God through the name of Jesus has made this man strong and healthy. You did not believe in Jesus when he was here, yet now you can see what we did in Jesus' name." *(Sway and say.)*

And Peter and John began to tell the people who were gathered around about Jesus. *(Sway and say.)*

## Supplies

beanbag or scarf

# Get Up and Walk

Have the children sit on the floor in a circle.

**Say: Let's play a game to remind you of today's Bible story. One person will walk around the outside of the circle, repeating "silver and gold" over and over. When that person comes to a person he or she wants to select, he or she drops the beanbag (or scarf) behind them and says, "Get up and walk." That person must then get up, pick up the beanbag, and go in the opposite direction around the circle walking. The object is for the person who is selected to beat the person who dropped the beanbag back to the empty place in the circle and sit down. The first one who reaches it, gets to stay there. The other person becomes the silver and gold sayer.**

Play the game with the children.

**Ask: Who in the story said, "Silver and gold I have none. But what I have I give to you."** *(Peter)* **What did Peter give the man instead?** *(the ability to walk)* **How did Peter do this?** *(through the healing power of Jesus)* **Peter shared his faith with the man who could not walk. How did he do this?** *(He used Jesus' power to heal him.)* **How do you think the man felt when Peter healed him?**

**Say: We may not be able to heal a person or do things such as the disciples did, but we can share our faith when we help others.**

## Supplies

None

# Sing the Story

Sing the following song with the children to the tune of "She'll Be Coming 'Round the Mountain."

O-o once there was a man who could
    not walk.
O-o once there was a man who could
    not walk.
On his bed he sat and cried
asking help from passersby.
O-o once there was a man who could
    not walk.

O-o John and Peter passed right by
    the man.
O-o John and Peter passed right by
    the man.
They stopped right at his bed,
and this is what they said.
"Now in the name of Jesus, stand
    and walk."

Then the man stood right up and
    jumped for joy.
Then the man stood right up and
    jumped for joy.
O he danced and he sang,
his praises loudly rang.
Then the man stood right up and
    jumped for joy.

Words: Daphna Flegal and LeeDell Stickler
Words © 1996 Abingdon Press

# Help Me, Please!

Photocopy and cut apart the Help Cards (**Reproducible 10A**) and Situation Cards (**Reproducible 10B**). Hand out the Help Cards to each child. Make sure every child has at least one. Place the Situation Cards in a basket.

**Say: I will read a situation card. You will look at your "Help Cards" and decide if you have the kind of help that is needed. If you think you do, then rush to the front and shout, "I can help!" You will then tell me how you can help.**

Read each situation slowly and carefully. If you have a large class, divide the children into groups of four to six. Provide a set of Help Cards for each table. Spread them out so that all the children can see them. Each table will select one child to be the runner. Only the runner can go to the front and shout.

Talk with the children about the different ways they can help others.

## We can help one another.

**Supplies**

Reproducibles 10A and 10B, scissors

# Helping Hand Prayers

Before class begins, draw around your hand on construction paper. Cut it out and draw a happy face on it. Tape the hand to a ruler or a folded piece of construction paper.

**Say: We can use our hands in so many different ways. We can clap.** (*Have the children clap their hands.*) **We can wave goodbye.** (*Have the children wave goodbye.*) **We can throw a ball.** (*Have the children pretend to throw a ball.*) **We can pick up our toys.** (*Have the children pretend to pick up toys.*) **We can give someone a pat on the back.** (*Have the children pat each other on the back.*) **We can help one another.** (*Have the children join hands.*) **Jesus taught his friends to help others. As we close today, I will pass the Helping Hand around. When it comes to you, I want you to share something you can do to help others this week.**

Pass the hand around the circle. When it has been all around the group, close with a prayer.

**Pray: Dear God, Jesus' friends spread the good news of Jesus by helping others. We can help others, too. Amen.**

**Supplies**

construction paper, scissors, felt-tip marker, ruler

**107**

**REPRODUCIBLE 10A**

ALL-IN-ONE BIBLE FUN

| Situation #1 | Situation #2 | Situation #3 |
|---|---|---|
| Sam fell down on the playground and scraped his knee. *(bandage)* | Jeff hit a tennis ball too hard. It went onto the roof and in the gutter. *(ladder)* | After school when Elizabeth came outside, it was raining very hard. *(umbrella)* |
| **Situation #4** | **Situation #5** | **Situation #6** |
| Mr. Wilson let a pan sit on the stove too long. It caught fire. Then his kitchen caught fire. *(fireman)* | Vicki wants to write a letter to her great aunt. She has a piece of paper. She needs something to write with. *(pencil)* | Mr. Alison is planting a flower garden. He has all the bedding plants ready to go in the ground. *(shovel)* |
| **Situation #7** | **Situation #8** | **Situation #9** |
| When Andy woke up this morning he didn't feel well. By lunch time he had lots of reddish spots all over his body. *(doctor)* | Amy Woo just came to this country. She speaks Chinese very well. But she wants to learn to speak English. *(teacher)* | The Smith family is on a camping trip. Mr. Smith wants to start the campfire so they can roast hot dogs. *(matches)* |
| **Situation #10** | **Situation #11** | **Situation #12** |
| While Mrs. Owen was driving to church, she ran over a nail. Soon her car was driving funny. *(mechanic)* | It rained and rained for many days. Soon the river overflowed its banks. Some families were stranded. *(rowboat)* | Mr. Banks has been out of work for almost a year. With no money coming in, it is hard to feed his family. *(box of food)* |
| **Situation #13** | **Situation #14** | **Situation #15** |
| During the day the air got colder and colder. It had been warm that morning. Now it is snowing. *(coat)* | After the big thunder storm, all the lights were out. *(flashlight)* | Lisa had been playing outside all afternoon. She was very thirsty when she came in the house. *(glass of water)* |
| **Situation #16** | **Situation #17** | **Situation #18** |
| Instead of sandwiches, the school served hot steaming bowls of vegetable soup. *(spoon)* | Hurricane Ella blew through the town. Many of the houses lost their roofs. *(hammer and nails)* | Drip, drip, drip. The faucet in the bathroom would not stop leaking. *(plumber)* |

**REPRODUCIBLE 10B** 109

Heroes of the Bible - Elementary
Permission granted to photocopy for local church use. © 1997, 2010 Abingdon Press.

# Dorcas

## Bible Verse

Trust in the LORD and do good.

Psalm 37:3

## Bible Story

Acts 9:36-42

Today's Bible story centers around a New Testament woman named Dorcas. Dorcas was a dressmaker who lived in the city of Joppa. "She was devoted to good works and acts of charity" (Acts 9:36). When she became ill and died, the followers of Jesus asked Peter to come to Joppa. Peter came, and Dorcas' friends showed Peter all the clothing Dorcas had made for them. Peter went to Dorcas and raised her from the dead. The news about Dorcas spread throughout Joppa, and many people became Christian as a result of this miracle. Dorcas was also known as Tabitha. She is the only woman in the Book of Acts to be identified as a disciple. "Now in Joppa there was a disciple whose name was Tabitha, which in Greek is Dorcas" (Acts 9:36).

The raising of Dorcas from the dead can lead to many questions for young children. They already have trouble understanding the concept of death. Young children view death as temporary and reversible. Answer the children's questions as honestly as you can. Remember that it is all right to say something like, "I don't know, but I do know that God loves us and always cares for us."

The emphasis for this lesson is on Dorcas' life of service. Dorcas was not a preacher or a teacher or an apostle, but she used the skills she had to the glory of God. She was a seamstress, making clothes for those in need.

Dorcas spent her time helping and giving to others. Young children can learn to freely help others. As a teacher, you can encourage children to make helping a habit by planning classroom routines such as cleanup; by offering opportunities for your children to do things for others; and by affirming children when they offer to help you or others.

# Disciples of Jesus do good to others.

If time is limited, we recommend those activities that are noted in **boldface**. Depending on your time and the number of children, you may be able to include more activities.

| ACTIVITY | TIME | SUPPLIES | |
|---|---|---|---|
| **What Should I Wear?** | **5 minutes** | **Reproducible 11A, crayons or felt-tip markers, construction paper, scissors** | JOIN THE FUN |
| Suit Up! | 10 minutes | bag of clothing | |
| Chain Reaction | 10 minutes | dominoes | BIBLE STORY FUN |
| Verse Scramble | 10 minutes | Reproducible 11B, scissors | |
| **Bible Story: Good Works by Dorcas** | **10 minutes** | **None** | |
| Crazy Couture | 10 minutes | masking tape, newspaper, scissors, accessories | |
| **Sign, Say, Pray** | **10 minutes** | **None** | LIVE THE FUN |

## Supplies

Reproducible 11A, crayons or felt-tip markers, construction paper, scissors

# What Should I Wear?

Make a copy of "What Should I Wear?" **(Reproducible 11A)** for each child.

Welcome the children as they come in. Comment on their clothing, as today's lesson tells about a woman who made clothing for the poor.

**Ask: Would you wear your pajamas to school? Would you wear a bathing suit to go snow skiing? Would you wear a jogging suit to a fancy dance?**

Give each child "What Should I Wear?" Encourage the children to match the person with the clothing.

**Say: Each of us has clothing that is special for what we want to do. But in Bible times clothing was much simpler. People had only the clothing they wore and perhaps some that was better for special occasions. Clothing was hard to come by because someone had to collect the fibers, spin it into thread, weave the thread into cloth, and then make the cloth into clothing. In today's Bible story, we learn about a woman who decided that as a follower of Jesus her job was to help make clothing for the poor.**

> ### Disciples of Jesus do good to others.

## Supplies

bag of clothing

# Suit Up!

Collect a large bag full of clean clothing. Include items such as hats, scarfs, mittens, sweaters, pants, skirts, ties, vests, and so forth. Make sure the clothing is large enough for even the largest child in your class.

Have the children sit in a circle.

**Say: Let's pretend that the bag of clothing we have here is the clothing that Dorcas, the woman in our Bible story today, has made for us. Pass the bag around. When I say, "Stop!" the person holding the bag will reach in and pull out an item of clothing, and put it on. Then we will start passing the bag again. Each time I say, "Stop!" the person who is holding the bag will put on an item of clothing. If you are caught with bag more than once, you get to put on another item of clothing.**

# Chain Reaction

**Supplies**

dominoes

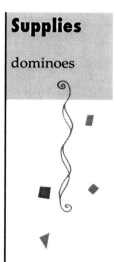

Set up dominoes on end in any pattern you like. They should be fairly close together. Once you have them all set up on end, gently push the first one and watch the chain reaction.

Say: Whenever we do something it causes a chain reaction, and you probably won't even know it. Sometimes that chain reaction is good; sometimes it's bad. When you help a pregnant woman carry something, it can make her feel better. Perhaps she will smile at someone because she feels better; perhaps then that person will feel better. If you yell at your brother, maybe he gets angry, and maybe he throws something at the dog. The dog can get hurt, and that can cause a trip to the vet, which makes your father get angry, and he yells at you about it.

Let the children take turns setting up the dominoes and watching the chain reaction.

Say: In our Bible story today, a woman named Dorcas does good things for other people. She definitely started a good chain reaction.

## Disciples of Jesus do good to others.

# Verse Scramble

**Supplies**

Reproducible 11B, scissors

Photocopy and cut apart the Scripture word cards (**Reproducible 11B**).

Read Psalm 37:3 to the children: "Trust in the LORD and do good."

Choose nine children to sit in a straight line facing the remaining children. Give each child one of the Scripture word cards in such a way that the verse is scrambled. Have the children hold the cards so that the remaining children can see them. If you have a small group of children give each child two or more consecutive cards.

Tell the remaining children that they will have to give instructions to the children with the Scripture word cards, so that they will know where to go in order to unscramble the verse. Instruct the children with the cards not to move until the other children give them instructions.

# Good Works by Dorcas

by LeeDell Stickler

Say: Today's Bible story tells us about a woman named Tabitha, whose Greek name was Dorcas. Dorcas was a follower of Jesus. We don't know if she ever met Jesus in person, but we do know she heard the stories and she believed. Because she believed, she turned her faith into doing good.

Teach the children the rap moves that go with the story poem. They will use this movement between the story stanzas.

**Rap:**
**Good works! Good works!** (*Hold right thumb in hitchhike position. Put left hand on the hips. As you move the thumb to the right, step two steps to the right in rhythm to the words.*)

**It's all about good works!** (*Reverse the moves above.*)

**It doesn't count if you don't turn,** (*Put hands on the hips and swivel hips to the right and to the left. Repeat one time.*)

**your faith into good works.** (*Pat left shoulder with right hand; leaving right hand on left shoulder, pat right shoulder with left hand; lean forward and pat left knee with right hand; while leaving right hand on left knee, pat right knee with left hand; stand upright; put right hand on the back side of right hip; put left hand on the back side of left hip.*)

Practice reading the story poem until you can read it in the rhythm.

There was a gal named Dorcas
She lived in Joppa-town
And nothin' bad that came around
Would get ole Dorcas down.

**Rap.**

To the seaport town of Joppa
Some people came one day.
They told about a special man
Who taught them of The Way.

**Rap.**

Now Dorcas listened carefully
To all the things she heard.
They told about the Son of God,
And she hung on every word.

**Rap.**

So Dorcas made a promise
To help in ways she could.
She'd use her skill at sewing,
Trusting God and doing good.

ALL-IN-ONE BIBLE FUN

**Rap.**

In and out her needle went
As Dorcas pulled the thread.
She helped the poor with every
stitch;
"Do for others," Jesus said.

**Rap.**

But one day unexpectedly
Our friend got sick and died.
All those that she had helped
before
Came to her house and cried.

**Rap.**

But one friend sent a message
Telling Peter to come quick.
He hurried to that little town;
He hadn't known that she was
sick.

**Rap.**

When Peter got to Joppa
He rushed to Dorcas' side.
He prayed to God to heal her,
Then she opened up her eyes.

**Rap.**

Then Peter, he reached down
to her,
And Dorcas took his hand.

Soon the story of the pow'r of God
Was told throughout the land.

**Rap.**

If you want to follow Jesus,
And Christians know they should,
Then take advice from Dorcas,
"Trust God and then do good."

# Crazy Couture

**Ask: In the story of Dorcas, how did she learn about Jesus?** *(from a group of people who had come to town who were followers of The Way)* **What did she decide to do?** *(become a follower of Jesus)* **How did she decide to help others?** *(make clothing for the poor)* **What happened to Dorcas one day?** *(She became ill and died.)* **Who helped her?** *(The people sent for Peter, who came and made her well again.)* **How do you think the people felt when they saw what happened?**

**Say: I'm sure Dorcas was very skilled with a needle and thread. When Dorcas made clothing she was sharing her gifts and talents. Let's create some special clothing.**

Divide the children into teams of two. One team member will be the model. The other team member will be the designer. Give each team newspaper, masking tape, scissors, and a variety of decorative items such as flowers, feathers, jewelry finds, and so forth.

**Say: Each team has ten minutes to create a one-of-a-kind outfit on the model. When everyone is finished we will have a fashion show with all our models.**

Have the models parade in front of the class. You may want to vote for the most creative costume.

**Say: Each of you have gifts and talents. It may not be designing paper clothing, but every one of you has some kind of talent.**

Encourage the children to think about their talents. Have each child name at least one talent.

**Ask: How can you use your talents to do good to others?** *(Look at the chart below for some suggestions.)*

| Talent | Doing Good |
| --- | --- |
| sewing | making clothes for others |
| sports | playing/teaching with younger children |
| music | playing an instrument/singing in worship |
| dance | dancing in worship |
| reading | reading to elderly/younger children |

**Disciples of Jesus do good to others.**

# Sign, Say, Pray

Have the children stand in a circle.

**Say: Disciples follow Jesus. Being a disciple of Jesus is a full-time job. It's not something we do on Sunday and then forget the rest of the week. Jesus is counting on us to be good disciples, and good disciples do good to others.**

Teach the children signs from American Sign Language for today's Bible verse.

**Trust** — Bring both hands slightly to the left, closing them to make fists ("S" hands). The right one should be slightly lower than the left.

**in** — Curl the left hand into a loose fist. Place the fingers of the right hand inside the left hand.

**the Lord** — Place the "L" sign at the left shoulder and then move it to the right waist.

**and** — Place the right hand in front of you, fingers spread apart and pointing left, palm facing you. Draw the hand to the right, closing the fingertips.

**do** — Place both "C" hands in front of you, palms down; move both hands to the right and left several times.

**good** — Touch the lips with the fingers of the right hand and then move the right hand forward, placing it palm up in the palm of the left hand.

Choose one child to step into the center of the circle.

**Say: (Child's name), you are a disciple of Jesus.**

Then have the remaining children in the circle sign and say the Bible verse together. Have the child in the center return to the circle.

Continue until every child has had the opportunity to be in the center of the circle and hear the Bible verse spoken to them.

**Pray: Thank you, God, for the disciples standing in this circle. Help them trust in you and do good. Amen.**

## Supplies

None

117

# What Should I Wear?

In today's Bible story, Dorcas makes clothing as an act of service. Look at the people here. Each one needs a special kind of clothing. Can you match the person with the clothing?

**REPRODUCIBLE 11A**

ALL-IN-ONE BIBLE FUN

| | | |
|---|---|---|
| **Trust** | **in** | **the** |
| **LORD** | **and** | **do** |
| **good** | **Psalm** | **37:3** |

Heroes of the Bible - Elementary

**All-in-One BIBLE FUN** ELEMENTARY

# Paul

## Bible Verse

Do not be afraid . . . for I am with you.

Acts 18:9-10

## Bible Story

Acts 9:1-22

The Bible story today comes from the Book of Acts. This book gives us a small peek at life among the early Christians. In this book we become acquainted with some of the early heroes and heroines of the New Testament. After Jesus' death, these men and women spread the good news of Jesus even as they fled from persecution.

In today's story the children will meet two of these heroes—Paul, who after his dramatic conversion, carried the Christian message to the Gentiles; and Ananias, the man whose courage set Paul on his course.

Paul was a devout Jew who thought the followers of Jesus were committing the most horrible sin—that of heresy. He received a special commission from the high priest in Jerusalem to arrest Christians wherever he found them and bring them back to Jerusalem for trial.

However, somewhere on his journey, Paul was blinded by a vision of Jesus. It was Ananias' touch that released Paul from his temporary blindness. How much courage it must have taken for Ananias to face Paul—who had come to Damascus to arrest him!

Adults often forget that young children have fears. To an adult the fear may seem insignificant. To a child, the fear can be overwhelming. Encourage the children to pray about their fears. Remind them that Jesus told them to not be afraid that he was with them always.

# We can ask Jesus for help when we are afraid.

If time is limited, we recommend those activities that are noted in **boldface**. Depending on your time and the number of children, you may be able to include more activities.

| ACTIVITY | TIME | SUPPLIES |
|---|---|---|
| **Alligator Swamp** | **10 minutes** | **Reproducible 12A, masking tape, yarn** |
| Risk It! | 10 minutes | blindfold, unbreakable object from the room such as a block, a box of crayons or a book |
| Hard and Easy | 10 minutes | foam balls or balls made from crumpled paper |
| Brother? Sister? | 10 minutes | blindfold |
| **Bible Story: Paul and Ananias** | **10 minutes** | **None** |
| Truth or Lie | 5 minutes | ball |
| Sing the Story | 5 minutes | None |
| Ready, Set, Draw! | 10 minutes | Reproducible 12B, scissors, crayons or felt-tip markers, large sheet of paper, basket or box |
| **Prayer Wave** | **5 minutes** | **None** |

JOIN THE FUN

BIBLE STORY FUN

LIVE THE FUN

## Supplies

Reproducible 12A, masking tape, yarn

# Alligator Swamp

Before class: Using masking tape or yarn, create a narrow path about twelve inches wide through the room. Photocopy the alligator picture (**Reproducible 12A**) and tape several along the outside of the path.

**Say: In order to come into the room today, you have to walk through the alligator swamp. There is a small path, it is very narrow. You have to walk very carefully in order to keep from being eaten by alligators.**

As the children tentatively walk the path, say things like: Oh, please be careful. Watch out! Watch where you put your feet. I'm afraid! Aren't you? Create a pretend atmosphere of fear and anxiety.

**Ask: How did it feel to have to walk through alligators to come into the class today? Would you like to really do this? Why not? Why are you afraid of alligators?** *(They are dangerous animals.)* **Are there other things that you're afraid of?** *(Invite the children to share, but do not insist on it.)*

> **We can ask Jesus for help when we are afraid.**

## Supplies

blindfold, unbreakable object from the room such as a block, a box of crayons or a book

# Risk It!

Select one child to be IT. The rest of the children form a circle around IT. Put a blindfold on IT. Place an object from the room at the feet of IT.

**Say: The object of the game is for someone from the circle to get the object and bring it back to the circle without getting caught. In order to catch the thief, IT must shout, "Stop, thief!" when IT thinks someone has the object. If someone has the object when IT shouts, that person then becomes IT.**

The teacher will touch someone on the shoulder. That is the person who will try to get the object. More than one person can try for the object.

When the game is over, have the children come to the storytelling area and sit down.

**Ask: How did it feel to be the one trying to steal the (name of object)? Were you afraid? Did you think you might get caught? What kind of feelings did you have? Can you think of other times when you feel this way— when you are not playing a game? Did you know that during those times, you can ask Jesus to help you not be afraid?**

# Hard and Easy

## Supplies

foam balls or balls made from crumpled paper

Pair the children. Give one child a foam ball. Or make balls by crumpling paper together into a ball shape. Have the other child form a hoop with his or her arms in front. Have the child with the foam ball stand back about six to eight feet and try to throw the ball into the hoop. The child forming the hoop cannot move. After several tries, have the two children swap.

After both children have had an opportunity to try to sink the basket, stop the game.

**Say: Now I want the one who is forming the hoop to help out and make sure that the ball goes through.**

Give the children a few minutes to try this. Then have them swap again. After both children have tried, gather the children together in a circle.

**Ask: Which was easier, trying to hit the hoop that stayed very still or trying to hit the hoop when the person is trying to help? Can you think of other things that are easier when someone helps?** *(cleaning your room, doing dishes, washing the car, doing homework, putting together a puzzle)*

**Say: Almost any task is easier when you have help. Today we are going to learn that Jesus can help us when we have difficult things to do.**

# Brother? Sister?

## Supplies

blindfold

**Say: In our Bible story we'll hear about two men, Saul and Ananias. Saul was going to Damascus to hurt anyone who was a follower of Jesus. While he was traveling he saw a bright light and heard Jesus speaking to him. Saul was blinded by the light and had to be led into the city.**

**Ask: How would you feel if something like that happened to you?**

**Say: Jesus told the other man in our story, Ananias, to go and help Saul. Ananias knew that Saul was hurting Jesus' followers, but he trusted Jesus. Ananias went to Saul and called him "brother." Saul was blind and could not see who was calling him.**

Blindfold one of the children to be Saul. Have the other children stand in a circle in an open area.

Quietly point to one of the children in the circle to be Ananias. Have Saul ask, "Where are you my brother, my sister?" Have Ananias answer, "I, your (sister or brother) am here." Saul should move toward the voice until he or she can gently touch the person. Saul should repeat the question and hear the response as often as needed. When Saul touches Ananias, that child becomes Saul.

**123**

# Paul and Ananias

by LeeDell Stickler

**Say: In today's Bible story, there is a character who is called upon to do something that is very dangerous for him. His name is Ananias. Can you say his name? He is asked to go and help someone who is his sworn enemy. He doesn't know what's going to happen. He has a special part in the story. We're going to act out what he says.**

Teach the children the Jazzy Walk. (This has a slightly rap feel to it.)

**1. I shoulda said, "Uh uh."**
Jazzy walk twice to the right. (*Step together step with right foot. Arms bent at elbows. Push forward as you step each time. Repeat.*)

**I shoulda said "Oh, no!"**
Jazzy walk twice to the left.

**2. I shoulda said, "I'm busy, Lord."**
Jazz roll. (*Roll arms around each other as you bend over. Reverse roll as you straighten up.*)

**3. "Get someone else to go."**
Fold arms across chest and shake head from left to right.

Practice several times with the children until they can do it easily.

Ananias mumbled to himself all the way down the busy Damascus street. It was very early in the morning. The market vendors were just beginning to set out their wares. But Ananias didn't notice. He just walked faster and faster.

*[Do the Jazzy walk.]*

Now, if anyone were to ask Ananias how he was feeling, he would probably said that he was afraid. Last night in a vision the Lord Jesus had appeared to him. "Ananias," Jesus had said, "I have something important for you to do. There is a man here in town who needs you. He has come from

ALL-IN-ONE BIBLE FUN

Jerusalem. His name is Saul. Get up and go to the house of Judas where he is staying. He is waiting for you. As he waits, he is fasting and praying because he is now blind. He is waiting for you to touch him."

*[Do the Jazzy walk.]*

"Lord," Ananias had said, "a lot of people have told me about this man. He has done terrible things to your followers in Jerusalem. *(Put hands to face.)* I had heard that the priests had given him the power to come here now and arrest anyone who worships in your name." Ananias was a follower of Jesus. He wondered what would happen when Saul discovered who HE was.

*[Do the Jazzy walk.]*

"Saul is the one I have chosen to tell foreigners, kings, and the people of Israel about me." And so Ananias knew that Jesus would be with him, and he went to find Saul.

*[Do the Jazzy walk.]*

Ananias walked up the path to Judas' house and then inside. *(Pat knees with hands, very slowly.)* There was Saul—sitting, praying, and waiting—waiting for Ananias. So Ananias placed his hands on Saul's face. *(Reach forward and pretend to touch a person's face.)* Suddenly, Saul could see again! He jumped up from his seat and shouted out, "Praise the Lord. Today I believe. I want to be a follower of Jesus!"

Ananias baptized Saul and took him to meet the other followers of Jesus who lived in Damascus. Saul told everyone what had happened on the road to Damascus.

"A bright light flashed around me and I had heard Jesus speaking to me," said Saul. "I was blinded by the light and my friends had to lead me into the city. I waited three days. Then Ananias came to me, called me brother, and touched my eyes. Suddenly I could see again!"

Saul told everyone that Jesus had changed his life forever.

*[Do the Jazzy Walk. Change the poem to reflect the following:]*

**I'm glad I didn't say, "Uh uh."**
**I'm glad I didn't say, "No."**
**Thank you for the courage, Lord,**
**It took for me to go.**

From that day on, Saul, or Paul as he was known in Greek, spread the word of Jesus everywhere he went.

## Supplies

ball

# Truth or Lie

Have the children sit in a circle on the floor.

Say: I am going to give a fact about something that might or might not have happened in today's story. Then I will roll the ball to someone. You will say either *truth*—if the fact is true or *lie*—if the fact is false.

Use these facts or make up some of your own.

Ananias was going to visit his mother.
On his way to Damascus, Saul had fallen off his horse.
Jesus sent Ananias to help Saul.
Saul had come to Damascus to arrest Christians.
Ananias was glad to go and help Saul.
When Saul regained his sight, he arrested Ananias.
Saul is also known by the name Paul.
Saul had been chosen to bring the good news of Jesus to foreigners.
Because of Ananias and Paul, no one knows about Jesus today.

After each response have the children roll the ball back to you.

## Supplies

None

# Sing the Story

Ask: How do you think Saul felt when he saw the bright light and heard the voice of Jesus? How do you think Ananias felt when Jesus told him to help Saul?

Say: Even though Saul and Ananias were probably afraid, they trusted that Jesus would be with them and help them.

> # We can ask Jesus for help when we are afraid.

Sing the song printed below to the tune of "Twinkle, Twinkle, Little Star."

Saul was on the road one day,
When he heard Lord Jesus say,
"Saul why do you hurt my friends?
They know my love never ends.
Saul, believe I love you too;
I have work for you to do."

"Ananias, go to Saul,
He has listened to my call.
I want you to help him see
And teach him to follow me.
Ananias, do not fear,
As you go I will be near."

**126**

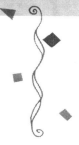

# Ready, Set, Draw!

**Supplies**

Reproducible 12B, scissors, crayons or felt-tip markers, large sheet of paper, basket or box

Photocopy and cut apart the fear cards (**Reproducible 12B**). Place the cards in a basket or box.

Say: **Everyone has times when they are afraid. Some people are afraid of things that others are not.**

Invite the children to gather around the large sheet of paper. Select one child to go first. He or she will draw a card from the basket or box. (If they need help reading what's on the card, whisper it in their ear.) They are then to try to draw on the paper what someone might be afraid of. They will begin drawing when you say, "Go." The rest of the group will try to guess it. The child that guesses gets to be the next drawer. Try to make sure every child has a turn.

Say: **Paul must have been afraid when he suddenly became blind. Ananias must have been afraid when he went to help Paul. What did we learn from the Bible story today?**

> **We can ask Jesus for help when we are afraid.**

# Prayer Wave

**Supplies**

None

Have the children sit in a circle.

Say: **Let's ask for Jesus help. I will name something that we might be afraid of. Then we will say together: "Please, Jesus, help me." After we have said that, we will have a wave—**(one person stands up and sits down. As that person sits down the next person stands up and sits down. As the second person sits down, the third person stands up, and so on around the circle.)

**Thunderstorms—Please, Jesus, help me!** (wave)
**Being left alone—Please, Jesus, help me!** (wave)
**Snakes—Please, Jesus, help me!** (wave)
**Performing in front of a group—Please, Jesus, help me!** (wave)
**Tests—Please, Jesus, help me!** (wave)
**The dark—Please Jesus, help me!** (wave)
(Invite the children to contribute their own fears.)

Pray: **Jesus, sometimes we are afraid. We are glad to know that when we are afraid, we can ask you to help us and you will be there. Amen.**

**127**

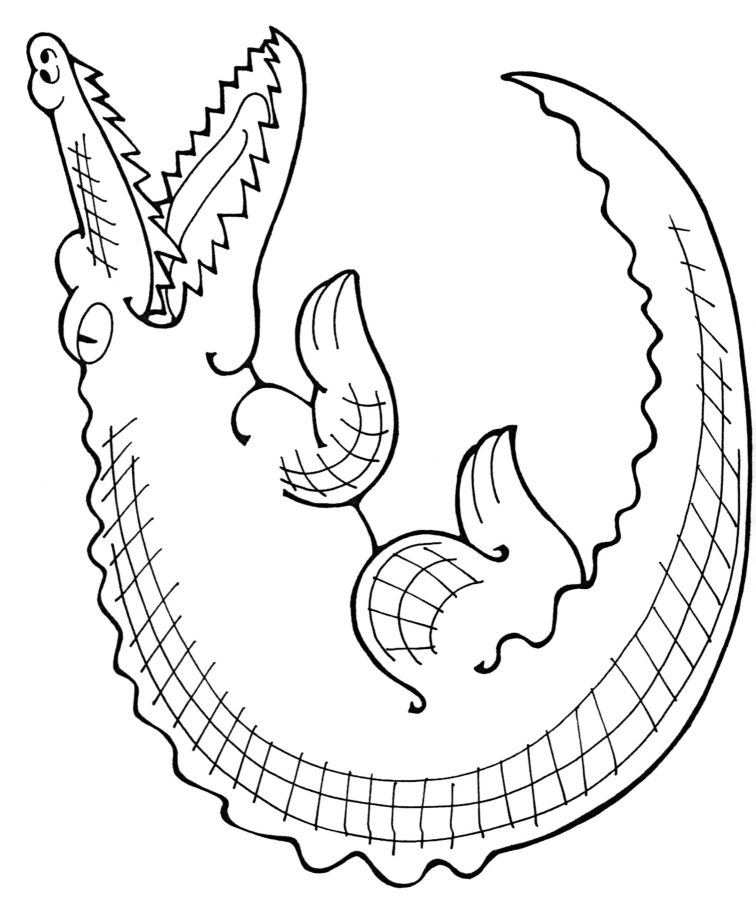

**REPRODUCIBLE 12A**

ALL-IN-ONE BIBLE FUN

| | | |
|---|---|---|
| **high places** | **storms** | **taking tests** |
| **going to the doctor** | **being left alone** | **getting lost** |
| **barking dogs** | **dark places** | **snakes** |
| **spiders** | **making a mistake** | **giving a report** |

# Lydia

## Bible Verse

We are ambassadors for Christ.

2 Corinthians 5:20

## Bible Story

Acts 16:6-15

During early New Testament times, there were Gentiles who believed in the one true God. Even though they were not Jewish, they observed the teachings of that faith. These Gentile believers were called God-fearers. When Paul brought the message of Jesus Christ to them, there were many converts.

A group of God-fearers lived in Philippi. As a Roman city, Philippi did not have a synagogue where the Jews could worship. In fact, it was against the law to worship God. Therefore, the God-fearers had chosen alternative places to worship—out of the way places where only believers would know what was happening. Paul, when he came to visit the city, sought out these meeting places.

Lydia, a merchant who sold purple cloth, was a God-fearer. She and a group of women met at the river to pray together. Lydia must have been a woman of wealth and some standing in the community. Purple cloth was expensive. The pigment

needed to create purple dye came from the secretions of mollusks. Each shell yielded only a small amount of dye. Only the wealthy could afford to own purple fabric. In fact, the phrase "the purple" referred not only to the color of the cloth but also to the class of people who could afford it.

When Lydia heard Paul's message, she became a believer. Because of her community standing, many people would have taken note of Lydia's decision and might even have followed in her footsteps. Lydia then offered Paul her home as a place to base his ministry while he was in Philippi.

Your children can become ambassadors for Christ just as Lydia and Paul were. Just because they are children does not make them any less important as members of Christ's church. There are many ways they can deliver the message of Jesus to other people.

# We can tell others about Jesus.

If time is limited, we recommend those activities that are noted in **boldface**. Depending on your time and the number of children, you may be able to include more activities.

| ACTIVITY | TIME | SUPPLIES |
|---|---|---|
| Similarities | 5 minutes | Reproducible 13A, scissors, purple crayon or marker |
| **Experiment With Color** | **10 minutes** | **watercolor paints, watercolor paper, brushes, containers of water, table covering, paint smocks** |
| Pass the Good News | 10 minutes | yarn, shower curtain rings or large metal washers |
| Good News Gossip | 5 minutes | None |
| **Bible Story: Paul and Lydia** | **10 minutes** | **guest to portray Lydia, purple cloth for headdress, Bible-times costume** |
| Spread the Good News | 10 minutes | Reproducible 13B, masking tape, table, paper, scissors, crayons or felt-tip markers |
| Hot Potato Bible Verse | 5 minutes | paper ball made earlier |
| **Sing and Pray** | **5 minutes** | **None** |

JOIN THE FUN

BIBLE STORY FUN

LIVE THE FUN

## Supplies

Reproducible 13A, scissors, purple crayon or marker

# Similarities

Before class: Photocopy and cut apart the pictures cards **(Reproducible 13A)**. On the last two cards, use a purple crayon or marker to color the fabric and the robe the woman is wearing.

Greet the children as they come into the room. Gather the children around a table.

**Say: I am going to put pictures of two items on the table. I want you to try to discover the connection between them. Sometimes it will be easy. Sometimes it will be hard.**

Use these combinations: horse/flower *(living things)*, bicycle/car *(wheels)*, flower/perfume *(smell good)*, tree/flower *(plants)*, chair/horse *(four legs)*, ball/bicycle *(roll)*, moon/lamp *(give light)*, horse/bicycle *(ride)*, wooden chair/tree *(wood)*. For the last combination, put down Lydia and the purple fabric *(purple)*.

**Say: In today's Bible story, this woman becomes a believer in Jesus Christ and makes it possible for others to hear the good news.**

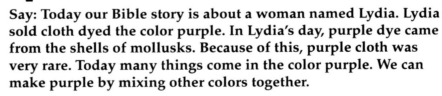

## We can tell others about Jesus.

## Supplies

watercolor paints, watercolor paper, brushes, containers of water, table covering, paint smocks

# Experiment With Color

**Say: Today our Bible story is about a woman named Lydia. Lydia sold cloth dyed the color purple. In Lydia's day, purple dye came from the shells of mollusks. Because of this, purple cloth was very rare. Today many things come in the color purple. We can make purple by mixing other colors together.**

**Say: Red, yellow, and blue are primary colors. All other colors are made from these three. The secondary colors of green, orange, and purple are made by mixing two primary colors together. Blue and yellow make green. Yellow and red make orange. Red and blue make purple. Various shades of these colors can by created by mixing different amounts of primary colors.**

Cover the table and have the children wear paint smocks. Give each child a piece of watercolor paper (or plain drawing paper). Let the children share the watercolor paints. Encourage the children to experiment mixing watercolors to make a purple picture on their papers.

# Pass the Good News

yarn, shower curtain rings or large metal washers

Have the children form a line, one beside the other with about three feet of space between each child, if possible. Give the first child in the line the end of the yarn. Unwind the yarn until it reaches the end of the line. Then let each child hold onto the yarn.

**Say: The object of this game is to get the rings from the first person in line to the last person in line. When all the rings have reached the end, reverse it. There is only one catch. You can't touch the ring with your hands. You can only hold onto the yarn. One hand must be touching the yarn at all times.**

The children will start when you say, "Go!" As the first ring makes its way down the yarn, start another one.

**Ask: Was it easy to move the rings? What made it easy?** *(Everyone working together.)*

**Say: Today's Bible story is about a man who had a special message and a woman who helped him spread the message. The man's name is Paul. The woman's name is Lydia. Together they helped tell others about Jesus.**

## We can tell others about Jesus.

# Good News Gossip

None

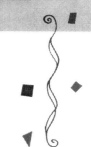

Have the children sit in a circle either on the floor or in chairs. Play a game of good news gossip. Begin a statement that tells about Jesus. Let the children whisper the statement to the person next to them. That person will then whisper it to the person next to him or her. The only rule is that once you have told the statement, you can't repeat it.

Use statements such as: Jesus was born in Bethlehem, Jesus said to love one another, Jesus healed the sick, Jesus is God's only Son.

Remind the children that it is important to pass the message on as correctly as possible. You may have only one chance.

# Paul and Lydia

by LeeDell Stickler

> Have someone from the church dress as Lydia and come to tell the Bible story. Have the guest wear a purple cloth as a headdress. If this is not possible, use a purple head scarf to create the image and tell the story dramatically.

My name is Lydia. I lived in the city of Philippi—a long, long time ago. And there I met a man named Paul. This man Paul changed my life forever. Let me tell you the story.

I am a merchant. I sell cloth. Not just any cloth, but purple cloth. Purple cloth is very expensive. Only the most important people can afford to buy my cloth. For that reason, I am a very important person too. Like all important people, everyone looks up to me. I must be very careful what I do.

Philippi is a Roman city, ruled by Roman law. The people there worship the Roman gods. Do you know that it is even against the law for people to worship any other gods?

But I believe in the one true God. For that reason, there is no place in Philippi for me to worship. There are other people in Philippi who believe as I do. We don't want to get arrested, so we worship in a very private place so that the Roman officials cannot find us and arrest us. We are going to worship God no matter what the law says.

So, every sabbath, these women and I gather to worship God and pray on the bank of the river. We have been doing this for a very long time. But one sabbath something strange happened.

A man named Paul came to our town. He was also a believer in the one true God. He asked people where he might find a group that worshiped God. Some people told him about our group down by the river.

That sabbath Paul came to our group. He told us who he was. He

ALL-IN-ONE BIBLE FUN

also said he had a very special message for us.

Paul began to tell us the story of Jesus. He told us how God had sent Jesus into the world to teach people more about God. He told us how Jesus had healed the sick and even raised the dead. He told us how Jesus had been arrested and put to death on a cross. He also told us how, on the third day, God had raised Jesus from the dead.

Paul told us how he had once been sent to Damascus to arrest the followers of Jesus. He told us how Jesus had appeared to him on the road and had changed his life forever.

The more Paul talked about this man Jesus, the more I knew that I believed too. "God has opened my heart to what you have said. I want to be a follower of Jesus too. Will you baptize me and my whole household?" I asked Paul.

I brought my whole family to the river that day. There Paul baptized us. Afterwards I invited Paul to stay at my house while he preached the good news in Philippi. The story of Jesus was truly on the move. I told my friends and family. Perhaps they will tell others too.

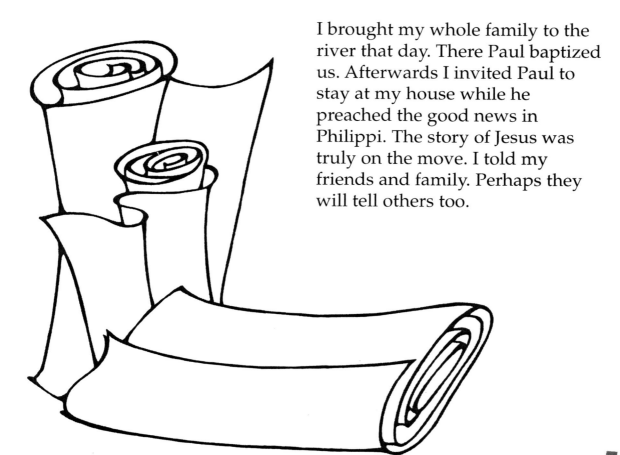

**135**

## Supplies

Reproducible 13B, masking tape, table, paper, scissors, crayons or felt-tip markers

# Spread the Good News

Photocopy the obstacles **(Reproducible 13B)**. Cut the obstacles apart and fold the bases on the dotted lines to make wickets.

Attach the wicket shapes around the table creating an obstacle course of wickets. Position the wickets so that the children can progress down the table, but do not put them in a straight line.

Once positioned, tape the bases down so that the breeze caused by the children blowing will not relocate them. Make sure the wicket is high enough to allow a paper ball pass easily.

Give each child a piece of paper.

**Say: We heard how Paul told Lydia the good news about Jesus. We heard how Lydia told her family the good news about Jesus.**

**Ask: Who are some of the people you can tell about Jesus?** *(Read the suggestions on the wickets.)* **What are some ways you can tell about Jesus?** *(tell a friend at school, invite a friend to church, read a Bible story to a younger child, write a card or letter, and so forth)*

Have the children write down at least one way they can tell others about Jesus. Or have the children draw a picture.

Have the children crumple the paper into a tight ball. The children will blow on the balls to make them move. Each ball must go through all the wickets in order to cross the finish line. If a ball blows off the table, reposition it at the place where it blew off.

If you have a large class, make several tables. Children may play in groups of two to four.

**Say: The object of the game is to get the good news ball from one end of the table to the other without it falling off. You must go through each obstacle, but you can't touch the ball with your hand. You must move the ball by blowing on it. If the ball blows off the table, you may set it back on the table at the position where it blew off and continue.**

## We can tell others about Jesus.

**136**

# Hot Potato Bible Verse

**Supplies**

paper balls
made earlier

Say: In our country we have ambassadors. These are people that we send to live for a time in another country. These people help the people of that country know more about us and help us to know more about them. When we are ambassadors for Christ, then we can help people know more about Jesus and how Jesus wants us to live.

Say: We're going to pass one of our paper balls around the circle. As you get the paper ball, you will say the next word in the Bible verse. Let's say the Bible verse together: "We are ambassadors for Christ" (2 Corinthians 5:20).

Using a paper ball made in the "Spread the Good News" activity, start the paper ball around the circle.

Say: Paul was an ambassador for Christ. He told Lydia the good news. Lydia became an ambassador for Christ. You can be an ambassador for Christ, too.

## We can tell others about Jesus.

# Sing and Pray

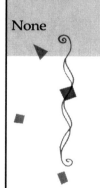

**Supplies**

None

Sing the song printed below with the children. The tune is "Down by the Riverside."

I know Paul met Lydia
down by the riverside,
down by the riverside,
down by the riverside.
I know Paul met Lydia
down by the riverside,
down by the riverside.


I know Paul told Lydia
down by the riverside,
down by the riverside,
down by the riverside.
I know Paul told Lydia

down by the riverside,
that Jesus showed God's
love.

I know Paul baptized Lydia
down by the riverside,
down by the riverside,
down by the riverside.
I know Paul baptized Lydia
down by the riverside,
and went to her house that day.

Words : Doris Willis
Words © 1986 Graded Press

Go around the group and let each child think of someone he or she can tell the good news about Jesus.

Pray: Dear God, thank you for opportunities to tell others about Jesus. Help us be ambassadors for Christ. Amen.

**REPRODUCIBLE 13A**

ALL-IN-ONE BIBLE FUN

People who don't know Jesus.

People who don't want to be different.

People who live far away.

People who don't want to change.

People who need to see to believe.

People who are set in their ways.

People who live across the ocean.

People who are afraid.

People who

# All-in-One BIBLE FUN

## Are you

- Feeling the budget pinch in your children's ministry?

- Unsure of the number of children you'll have in Sunday school each week?

- Working with a Sunday school program that doesn't meet each week?

LET THE FUN BEGIN

Order Today!

# Preschool

# Elementary

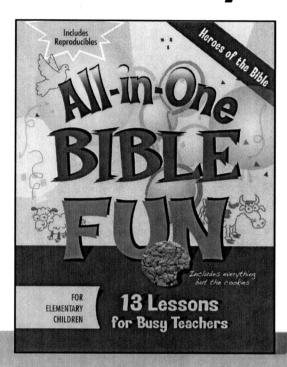

## All-in-One Bible Fun

is available for preschool- and elementary-age children. Each book will focus on a specific theme:

- *Stories of Jesus*
- *Favorite Bible Stories*
- *Fruit of the Spirit*
- *Heroes of the Bible*

- Thirteen complete lessons in each book
- No additional components to purchase
- Each book includes lesson plans with your choice of arrival activities, a Bible story, a Bible verse and prayer, and games and crafts
- Material is undated so teachers can use the books throughout the year

## All-in-One Bible Fun: 13 Lessons for Busy Teachers

Stories of Jesus—Preschool 978-1-426-70778-0
Stories of Jesus—Elementary 978-1-426-70779-7

Favorite Bible Stories—Preschool 978-1-426-70783-4
Favorite Bible Stories—Elementary 978-1-426-70780-3

Fruit of the Spirit—Preschool 978-1-426-70785-8
Fruit of the Spirit—Elementary 978-1-426-70782-7

Heroes of the Bible—Preschool 978-1-426-70784-1
Heroes of the Bible—Elementary 978-1-426-70781-0

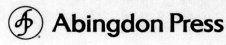

**Abingdon Press**

abingdonpress.com | 800-251-3320

# One Room SUNDAY SCHOOL ®

## Working with a broader age group?

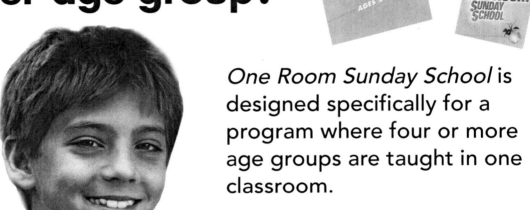

*One Room Sunday School* is designed specifically for a program where four or more age groups are taught in one classroom.

**For children age 3 through middle school!**

Students will grow together through comprehensive Bible study, application of Bible lessons to everyday discipleship, and a variety of age-appropriate activities.

 Abingdon Press

**Hear, See, and Live Your Belief in God**

# Live B.I.G.'s
# One Big Room

## A Proven Sunday School Program for Mixed-Age Group Children's Ministries

kit includes everything you need for the quarter

- 3 DVDs
- One Music CD
- One Leader Book

*For children age 3 through middle school!*

Abingdon Press

CPSIA information can be obtained at www.ICGtesting.com
Printed in the USA
LVOW09s2007180214

374248LV00001B/2/P